The Decorated Tree

The Decorated Tree

RECREATING TRADITIONAL CHRISTMAS ORNAMENTS

By Carol Endler Sterbenz and Nancy Johnson
Text by Gary Walther

Harry N. Abrams, Inc.,
Publishers, New York

For Mom and Dad, who
helped me believe that anything is possible
C. E. S.

For Jimmy, Dennis, Adrienne, and Juliet
N. J.

PROJECT MANAGER   PROJECT EDITOR   DESIGNER
Pegg Nadler   Margaret Donovan   Darilyn Lowe

Technical Writer   Technical Artist   Photographer   Photo Stylist
Linda Macho   Janet Aiello   Bob Hanson   Emily Leeser

Library of Congress Cataloging in Publication Data
Sterbenz, Carol Endler.
   The decorated tree.
   Summary: Presents the history and tradition associated
with the Christmas tree and provides illustrated
instructions for making tree ornaments for ten different
motifs.
   1. Christmas decorations. [1. Christmas trees.
2. Christmas decorations. 3. Handicraft] I. Johnson,
Nancy. II. Walther, Gary. III. Title.
TT900.C4S727   745.594′1   82-1774
ISBN 0-8109-0805-0   AACR2

© 1982 Harry N. Abrams, Inc.

Published in 1982 by Harry N. Abrams, Incorporated, New York
All rights reserved. No part of the contents of this book may be
reproduced without the written permission of the publishers

Printed and bound in the United States of America

Table of Contents

Introduction

For more than four centuries now, the decorated tree has delighted the human spirit at Christmas. Although it is not clear exactly how and when the evergreen became associated with the holiday, there are some wonderful popular legends explaining the origin of the custom. One describes how on the evening of Christ's birth, a multitude of trees and flowers, each wearing its most colorful bloom, assembled before the manger in Bethlehem to pay homage to the Savior. Standing bashfully apart was an evergreen, which, because its needles never changed color or blossomed, felt it had nothing special to offer. Some of the stars, taking pity on the tree's plight, descended from the heavens and settled in its branches, transforming the evergreen into the brightest member of the colorful cast. When he saw the dazzling evergreen, the Christ Child reached out in joy, and ever since, concludes the legend, the tree has played a special role at Christmas.

In fact, the use of evergreens in religious rituals is older than Christmas itself. The Bible gives no date for Christ's birth, and it was not until the year 320 that the Catholic Church decided upon December 25 as the day on which that miracle would be commemorated. But long before then, pagan tribes living in northern Europe had come to regard the evergreen as a symbol of everlasting life because its branches never shed. During the feast of the winter solstice—that pivotal moment in darkest December when the days, imperceptibly at first, begin to lengthen—Germanic tribes decorated their rude dwellings with evergreen branches. Also called the feast of the unconquered sun, this celebration marked the return of light to the world, and to the pagan mind represented the pushing back of the forces of darkness.

The first decorated Christmas tree we know of, called the Paradise Tree, was used as a theatrical prop. It represented the Garden of Eden in the medieval mystery play about the fall of Adam and Eve, which was usually performed on December 23. Mystery plays died out around 1650, but by then people living along the Rhine River in present-day Germany and France had already begun decorating evergreens. From there the tree has taken root in most of the colder northern areas of Europe and North America. (Decorated evergreens have never been popular in Spain and Italy, and Mexico and South America have developed their own colorful Christmas customs, such as the piñata, which do not involve the tree.)

Along the way the decorated tree has had its ups and downs. More than one person has denounced it as a barbarous custom unsuitable for Christ's birthday, but most people have found it enchanting, and an astonishing variety of objects have hung upon its branches. Evergreens have held everything from unconsecrated Communion wafers to Mickey Mouse decals and have often reflected the concerns of the people decorating them. The earliest trees, such as the Christbaum, were decorated with little more than Communion wafers and polished apples, an indication of the essentially religious nature of the Christmas celebration in the sixteenth and seventeenth centuries. In the late nineteenth century, by contrast, a goodly number of ornaments shaped like hot-air balloons began turning up on Christmas trees, reflecting the hold lighter-than-air flight held for the public at the time.

Some outlandish trees have been improvised with quite humorous results. In 1900, for example, a group of University of Pennsylvania biology students played a Christmas prank by presenting their instructor with a fir tree that contained, among other things, long strings of vertebrae arranged from an evolutionary standpoint; preserved specimens of bugs, beetles, and fish; a stuffed monkey or two; and stuffed birds guarding nests full of eggs. In 1897 James Clements and his wife put up an evergreen in their New York hotel room and decorated it with $70,000 worth of gold nuggets, which Clements had found that year while prospecting in the Klondike. And in the 1920s the SPCA of Boston adorned Post Office Square with a tree hung with apples and lumps of sugar for the few horses still used as draft animals.

Like the rest of western society, the tree has become increasingly secular during the past four hundred years, but especially since the 1880s. About that time, people began to favor durable ornaments such as Christmas balls and tiny cardboard musical instruments over edible ornaments, which had formerly made up most of the decorations on the tree. Ornaments have changed, too, from handmade and homemade to manufactured and store-bought—which brings us to the real subject of this book.

In his memoir *Prairie Christmas*, Paul Engle describes Christmas at the turn of the century on his family's farm. "It was a handmade Christmas. The entire family either sewed, whittled, knit, sawed, crocheted, embroidered, baked, pasted, or cracked to celebrate the generous days with gifts." A similar feeling animates this book—the desire to make a special effort for the holidays, the Christmas spirit that finds an outlet in handcrafting ornaments.

Each chapter tells the story of a decorated tree and the people who created it. More than just an introduction to the great family of decorated trees, the book focuses on the rich rewards of hand-crafting the Christmas decorations that made yesterday's trees so special. For more than a year Carol Sterbenz and Nancy Johnson have been rummaging through the history of Christmas ornaments as if it were an attic trunk full of long-forgotten but wonderful objects. They have selected seventy-eight ornaments from Christmases past and provided clear, concise instructions for making them. In some cases they have adapted the original ornament to modern materials; in others they have given free rein to artistic inspiration and altered the design while remaining faithful to the original conception.

The result is a collection of ornaments that have engaging stories behind them, are absorbing to make, and will satisfy both beginners and experienced crafts-people. We also hope that the text, in describing some ornaments not covered in the crafts sections, will spark your own imagination and enthusiasm and prompt you to make some decorations on your own. Some of the most attractive trees pictured in this book were created in just that fashion, and it is a tradition worth continuing.

G.W.

Glossary

Backstitching: Strengthening the beginning and end of a seam by making several stitches forward and backward along the seamline.

Basting: Temporary stitches (about 1/4″ long and 1/4″ apart) done by hand or machine for a variety of purposes, e.g., to hold fabrics together or to gather an edge.

Beveling: Sanding the edge of a piece of wood at an angle, using medium, then fine sandpaper to form a slanted edge.

Bisque firing (also known as biscuit firing): Firing ware that has not been glazed as a final process, or firing ware to facilitate handling in the glazing process.

Bone dry: The condition of dried clay when there is absolutely no water left in the clay body; ware becomes lighter in color and cannot be worked. If any water remains in a clay body being fired, it will blow up in the kiln; "soaking" projects in a 100–150°F. oven overnight will ensure dryness.

Casing: A channel of fabric through which an elastic or drawstring is pulled.

Cone: A three-sided ceramic pyramid that will bend at a specific temperature in a kiln to record the progress of the work done by the heat.

Coping saw: A hand-held saw used for cutting curves and straight sections of wood.

Cross-hatching: Scoring a worked piece of clay with a trimming needle or knife to facilitate attaching it to another piece of clay. The score lines should intersect each other so that the surface is quite rough.

Facing: A second piece of fabric used to finish and conceal a raw edge. A facing is stitched to the original fabric with right sides together and raw edges even, then turned to the wrong side and pressed, making a smooth, finished edge.

Firing: Chemically changing a clay body or glaze through high heat in a kiln.

Grog: Granulated bisque ware that is added to a clay body to give it texture and strength.

Jig saw: A stationary saw that allows for interior and exterior sawing of curved, scrolled, or straight sections of wood; portable model also available.

Kiln: A furnace or oven used to fire clay and glaze.

Leather hard: The condition of partially dried clay when shrinkage has stopped and the surface has not become lighter in color; ware is still soft enough to turn or finish, yet firm enough to handle without fear of distortion.

Loop: A tool with a wooden handle and a thin, teardrop-shaped wire end for scooping and removing excess clay.

Overglaze: A final finish put on pottery.

Porcelain clay: A mechanically strong blend of materials that will become translucent upon bisque firing; the glaze on porcelain is usually fired at a very high temperature, making the piece hard and resistant to abrasion.

Quilling: The art of rolling thin strips of

paper into different shapes and using those shapes to create lacy designs.

Rapidograph pen: A technical fountain pen that uses India ink. Available in point widths from very fine (0000) to thick (9); #1 is suggested.

Scoring: In ceramics, making a slash in clay using a trimming needle or knife to facilitate the fusion of two worked pieces. In general crafting, making a cut in heavy paper or cardboard with an X-acto knife to facilitate easy bending of the paper or cardboard along the cut.

Seam allowance: The distance from the sewing line to the edge of the fabric (1/4″ for most projects).

Slip: A suspension of clay or glaze in water; indispensable for throwing, attaching pieces, and repairing cracks.

Soft sculpture: A fabric work, stuffed with batting or fiberfill, that can be transformed into a three-dimensional shape through stitching.

Stilts: Small ceramic or metal forms used in firing objects that cannot be fired flat; also used to prevent glazed areas from fusing to the floor of the kiln during firing.

Tack cloth: Cheesecloth dipped in varnish to make a sticky cloth; used for picking up particles of sanded wood before painting or varnishing, or for cleaning away particles of sanded varnish.

Template: A guide used for forming repetitive shapes, usually made from sturdy cardboard; coat edges of cardboard with clear nail polish to keep them hard.

Topstitching: Stitching above or below a seam on the right side of the fabric through all thicknesses.

Trimming needle: A large needle used to remove excess clay from the main body of a ceramic piece.

Underglaze: A decoration painted on clay that is either unfired or bisque fired; later it is covered with a transparent overglaze.

Wedging: Kneading and cutting clay to eliminate air and make it homogeneous and plastic.

General Directions

USE OF CANDLES

Do not use candles on trees. It is extremely hazardous.

For historical accuracy, we have photographed many of our trees with lighted wax candles. It must be stressed, however, that these are studio photographs taken with modern fire protection precautions. Candles should never be used on trees in the home; such use is an extreme fire hazard. It may also be illegal in some areas of the United States—your local fire inspector should be consulted.

Because of the many beautiful illustrations of historic trees, people today tend to think that candles blazed on household Christmas trees every evening through the twelve days of Christmas. The truth is that candles were lit for no more than a scant half hour, at most, on Christmas Eve. While the children gaped with joy, their parents stood by nervously with a bucket of water. Tragic incidents of fires caused by candles on trees were numerous and well known. Not until the development of electric Christmas lights could illuminated trees be enjoyed for long periods with little or no fire danger.

To avoid serious fire hazard, we strongly recommend the use of a non-flammable tree (or greens) or artificial candles; the latter are preferable since they avoid a flame altogether yet still impart a warm glow to the tree. If for some reason real candles must be used despite the risks, the following precautions are vital: the tree or evergreen boughs should be placed away from stairways and doorways, preferably in a corner; a Class B fire extinguisher containing dry chemicals should be near at hand; the candles should be lit once only, and then briefly; the candles should be snuffed rather than blown out.

TRANSFERRING DESIGNS

Materials: Paper for pattern. Graphite paper. Hard lead pencil or dry ball-point pen. Tape or straight pins.

Trace pattern as directed. Complete half patterns, indicated by long, heavy dash lines, by reversing the pattern and drawing the reversal next to the original, aligning the dash lines. Transfer design outlines as follows: Place working medium (paper, wood, fabric, etc.) right side up on work surface; place graphite paper face down over working medium. Center pattern over graphite and secure to working medium with tape or straight pins to prevent shifting. Trace around lines of design with a hard lead pencil or dry ball-point pen. Before removing tape or pins, carefully lift one corner of pattern and graphite to make sure the transfer is clear. If transfer is not clear, go over lines again; if clear, remove pattern and graphite paper. Proceed with the project following the individual directions.

CERAMICS

Materials: Commercially prepared, pre-wedged porcelain clay. Cones for firing (see package directions for cone numbers). Bowl of water. Q-tips or toothpicks. Sturdy cardboard and scissors for patterns, or cookie cutters. Trimming needle, darning needle, or heavyweight straight pins. Sable paintbrushes for underglaze, #0 and #3. Wire for hanging pieces in kiln while firing and for dipping ornaments into overglaze. *For Rolling Clay:* Damp cloth. Two lattice strips, desired thickness. Rolling pin. *See individual craft directions for additional materials.*

It is best to make twice the number of ornaments required because this is a delicate process, and cracking or breakage can occur in firing.

To roll clay to an even thickness, place clay on a damp cloth stretched between lattice strips of the desired thickness of the clay. Roll from center of clay outward, moving lattice strips as necessary. Wash rolling pin occasionally and wipe dry to prevent clay from sticking. Make sure flattened clay slab is free of tears or cracks.

Clay shapes can be made in two ways: by using a pattern or by using cookie cutters. To use pattern method, make a cardboard template of the desired pattern; position the template on flattened clay slab. Cut around template with trimming needle, darning needle, or straight pin to cut out clay shape; allow clay to stiffen slightly before removing excess to prevent stretching of cut shapes. To use cookie cutter, press cutter down firmly into the flattened clay slab; remove excess clay from around shape before lifting cutter. Make sure cutter is clean before using it a second time, or clay will stick to it.

After ornaments have been shaped following the individual craft directions, allow to dry leather hard or bone dry as directed (*see Glossary*). Apply underglaze, if required, using sable paintbrushes; fire underglaze in kiln to cone indicated on package directions.

To apply overglaze, run a wire through the hanging loop or hole of the ornament. Pass ornament quickly under water, then dip it in the overglaze. To prevent ornament from sticking to hanging rod in kiln during firing, use a wet toothpick or Q-tip to remove all overglaze from inside of hanging loop or hole. Attach ornament to hanging rod in kiln; fire to required cone. Attach string or ribbon to hanging loop or hole.

WOODWORKING

Materials: Sharp pencils. Cork-backed steel ruler. Masking tape. T- or carpenter's square. Carbon paper. Jig or coping saw. Medium and fine sandpaper. Tack cloth. Waterproof glue. *See individual craft directions for additional materials.*

Using a very sharp pencil and carbon paper held in place with masking tape, transfer pattern outlines to wood. Mark pattern pieces on wood with longest dimensions along grain; also mark curved edges along grain if possible. Use jig or coping saw to cut out pieces along marked lines as directed. Sand cut edges with medium, then fine sandpaper until smooth.

For figures, cut with jig or coping saw. Sand front and back of piece until smooth, always sanding with grain.

Paint or stain piece as directed for individual crafts; allow to dry thoroughly. Complete any other details necessary for each individual project, then give piece two or three coats of varnish back and front, unless otherwise directed. Allow to dry thoroughly between coats. Lightly sand smooth between coats with fine sandpaper for a super-smooth finish.

SEWING

Materials: *See individual craft directions.*

Most patterns and measurements include a $1/4''$ seam allowance, indicated on patterns by areas beyond dash lines. Bracketed arrows pointing to seam indicate that seam should be placed on fold. Solid line indicates hemline. Trace patterns as directed, then pin to suggested fabrics, and cut out along seamlines. Transfer dots, X's, or other markings to wrong side of fabric; transfer all embroidery lines to right side of fabric as follows: Center pattern over fabric with a piece of graphite paper in between and pin; trace pattern with tracing wheel, hard lead pencil, or dry ball-point pen. Remove pattern and tracing paper. When following measurements for pieces without patterns, mark lines or circles on fabric using ruler or compass, and cut out along marked lines; these measurements will always include a $1/4''$ seam allowance. If fabrics ravel, zigzag-stitch around raw edges, or pink them with pinking shears.

Complete all embroidery designs before sewing pieces together, unless other-

SLIP STITCH

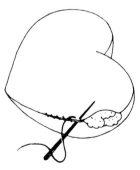

WHIP STITCH

wise directed. To sew, set stitch length on sewing machine for 10 to 12 stitches per inch. For basting, set stitch length for 6 to 8 stitches per inch. Sew two pieces together with right sides facing and raw edges even, making 1/4″ seams. Secure stitches by backstitching at beginning and end of each seam. If possible, always press seam allowances open. Clip into seam allowances at curves to ease stress.

For hand sewing, slip-stitch or whipstitch with small invisible stitches using matching thread.

EMBROIDERY

Materials: *See individual craft directions.*

Trace embroidery pattern. Transfer design to right side of fabric as follows: Place fabric right side up on work surface. Place a piece of graphite paper over fabric, then center pattern over fabric and paper. Pin. Trace around all design lines, using a hard lead pencil or dry ball-point pen. Remove pattern and graphite paper. Do not cut out design until after embroidery is complete, unless otherwise directed.

Stretch area to be embroidered in embroidery hoop to hold fabric taut; reposition hoop as necessary, and pull fabric taut in hoop if it begins to sag while working. Embroider design following individual directions.

Begin embroidering by leaving end of floss on back of fabric and stitching over it to secure; do not make knots. To end a strand or begin a new one, weave the floss under stitching on back. If floss begins to

kink or twist while you are embroidering, allow needle and floss to hang straight down to unwind.

When embroidery is complete, steam-press on padded surface.

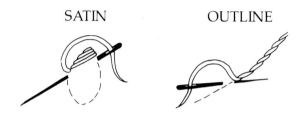

SATIN   OUTLINE

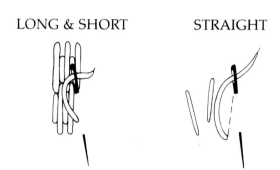

LONG & SHORT   STRAIGHT

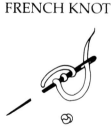

FRENCH KNOT

The Decorated Tree

The Paradise Tree

Imagine the square of a small northern European village in the middle of winter. In the center stands a stage, bare except for a ring of lighted candles surrounding a majestic fir, its boughs arching outward in graceful symmetry. The tree's decorations make it a symphony of Christmas colors: polished red apples and cherries hang from the branches; white wafers spangle the deep green needles like stars.

While this enchanting scene might well mystify us today, someone from the fifteenth century would recognize it immediately as the setting for the Paradise Play, a miracle play depicting the life of Adam and Eve in the Garden of Eden. The play was performed within the circle of lighted candles, and the decorated tree at its center—one of the earliest we know of—was called the Paradise Tree because it was the principal prop in the play.

Miracle plays were a form of religious instruction and popular entertainment during the Middle Ages. They dramatized episodes in the history of Christianity, and at a time when most people could neither read nor write, they were often the only means by which the Catholic Church could teach its doctrines. Encompassing both the Old and the New Testaments, they were arranged in cycles to correspond with feast days on the liturgical calendar. The cycle of miracle plays began with the story of the Creation and went on to show Adam and Eve in Paradise, the domestic quarrels of Noah and his bossy wife (which always provoked hearty laughter), and the stories of Cain and Abel, Moses, David, and King Solomon; they climaxed with the birth of Christ and the flight of Mary and Joseph into Egypt.

Simple at first, miracle plays grew more complex over time through the addition of dialogue and secular elements not mentioned in the Bible. Gradually the characters became more human, and the language in which the plays were performed changed from Latin to the vernacular. As they became more entertaining, the plays took on a rambunctious and sometimes ribald character, which provoked the ire of the Church. In 1210, Pope Innocent III forbade the clergy to act in them, perhaps thinking that his edict would mean fewer performances. It had no such effect. Rather the plays became more popular because the parts were now taken by ordinary people and groups of actors who traveled from town to town.

The story of Adam and Eve in Paradise was one of the most popular miracle plays. In the Middle Ages, the Church designated December 24 as Adam and Eve's feast day, and beginning in the twelfth century or thereabouts, it also became the day when the Paradise Play was performed.

Despite its sparseness, the stage—at least the area within the circle of candles—was intended to represent nothing less than the Garden of Eden. The Paradise Tree symbolized the two trees that stood at the center of the garden, the Tree of Life and the Tree of Knowledge of Good and Evil. Sometimes the actors made the connection explicit by standing a kind of medieval playbill against the tree in the form of a wooden cutout that showed Adam and Eve flanking a serpent coiled around the Tree of Knowledge. (As late as the nineteenth century, people in northern Germany still placed figures of Adam, Eve, and the serpent under their trees at Christmas.)

No one knows what kind of tree really stood at the center of the Garden of Eden. At various times theologians and scholars have suggested that it was a fig, a palm, or a pomegranate, but never a fir, and no one knows exactly why a fir was used in the Paradise Play. It may be because the tree was an evergreen and therefore a symbol of immortality. Then, too, the fir has long played an important role in ritual and legend, especially among the Germanic peoples of northern Europe, where the Paradise Tree first became a popular Christmas custom. For centuries, the pagans of northern Europe brought evergreens into their homes at the winter solstice, which falls at about the same time as Christmas, to celebrate the return of the sun and the defeat of the forces of darkness.

More directly related to the use of the fir in the Paradise Play is a legend concerning Saint Boniface, the English monk credited with bringing Christianity to Germany about A.D. 700. As the legend has it, under a mighty oak the saint came upon a group of pagans who were preparing to sacrifice their chieftain's son to Thor, the pagan god of thunder. Enraged, Boniface toppled the oak with one blow of his axe, whereupon the stunned pagans asked him for the word of God. Boniface pointed to an evergreen and told them to take it into their homes as the tree of the Christ Child.

Although everyone watching the Paradise Play knew its outcome—Adam and Eve are expelled from the Garden of Eden—the decorations on the Paradise Tree served to underscore the play's meaning. The apples symbolized the forbidden fruit and the Fall of Man, while the white wafers (unconsecrated Communion hosts) represented man's salvation through Jesus Christ. Their presence on the same tree was meant to show that while

God had condemned mankind to a life of toil on earth, He had also provided for its eventual salvation. The cherries were also a symbol of hope, having their origin as a decoration in an old Christian legend concerning the Annunciation. Joseph and Mary, as the story goes, were walking in a garden full of cherry trees when Mary told him about the visitation of the angel. Joseph didn't believe her, and soon after, when she asked him for some cherries, he refused to pick them, perhaps out of irritation. He was dismayed, however, to see the branches of the cherry trees bend low so that Mary could reach them. Placed on the tree, the cherries reminded the audience of the Annunciation and ad-monished them to have faith even when common sense might dictate otherwise.

The Church banned miracle plays in the fifteenth century, at the height of their popularity, to no avail. They finally died out a century later, but not before families had taken up the custom of decorating a Paradise Tree at Christmas, especially in the regions of present-day France and Germany lying along the Rhine River. Although the Paradise Tree fell by the wayside eventually—it was replaced by the Christbaum and the Lichtstock—it began a revolution in the way Christmas was celebrated that has continued for more than four hundred years.

WHITE WAFER

NOTE: Before beginning, read General Directions for Ceramics on page 14 for additional materials and directions.

Skill Level: Elementary.

Materials: Pre-wedged porcelain clay that fires to cone o6. Two 1/8″ lattice strips. White satin ribbon for hanging. Cross pendant or basswood stripping 1/8″ square. X-acto knife. White glue.

Directions: Trace pattern outline onto sturdy cardboard and cut out. Roll slab of clay between 1/8″ lattice strips. Use pattern to cut circle from clay; bore a hanging hole in ornament using trimming needle and following open circle on pattern for position. Emboss circle with a cross pendant by pressing the cross firmly into the clay. If you do not have a cross pendant, make a cross from basswood stripping as follows: Cut one 1 3/8″ length and two 3/8″ lengths. Glue 3/8″ pieces to each side of longer piece following pattern given on circle. Let dry, then press firmly into clay to emboss the cross. Allow to dry leather hard, then bisque-fire ornament to cone o6. Make a hanging loop with white satin ribbon and thread through hole.

NOAH AND THE ARK

NOTE: Before beginning Ark, read General Directions for Woodworking on page 15 for additional materials and directions.

Skill Level: Advanced.

Materials: *For All:* Plasmolegno or other wood modeling compound, about 2 lbs. Bowl of water. Aluminum foil. Hatpins and/or toothpicks. Fine sandpaper. Acrylic paints: colors shown in photograph. Paintbrushes, medium and fine. *For Noah:* 1/16″ dowel, 3 3/4″ long. *For Ark:* Basswood: 1/16 × 1/2 × 22″; 1/4 × 4 × 22″. Coping saw. Medium sandpaper. White glue.

Directions: *Ark:* Using patterns, cut one roof and two house ends from 1/4″ basswood. Measure and cut the following from 1/4″ basswood: one 4 × 2 1/4″ roof, one 7/8 × 1 3/8″ roof door (or use wood section remaining from cut-out pattern roof), two 3 × 2″ house sides, one 3/4 × 2″ door, one 3/4 × 1/2″ window, one 2 3/8 × 1 7/8″ window, one 7/8 × 4″ ladder. From 1/16″ basswood, cut six 5/8 × 1/4″ rungs.

Sand all pieces with medium, then fine sandpaper. Bevel one long edge of roof door so that when glued it will appear to be swinging open; see photograph. Glue beveled edge of door to left side of roof opening. Glue house ends between house sides with bottom edges flush and 90° angles at corners. Bevel

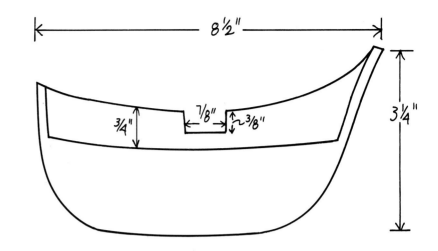

ARK SCULPTING DIAGRAM

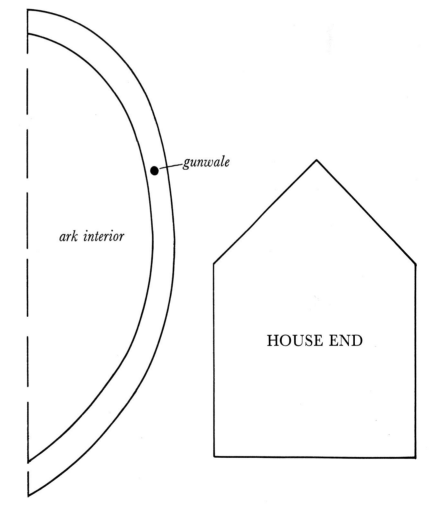

ark interior

gunwale

HOUSE END

ROOF

NOAH

ELEPHANTS

SCULPTING DIAGRAMS

GIRAFFES

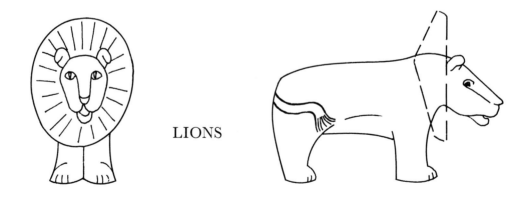

LIONS

upper edges of house sides, continuing the slant of the house ends. Glue rectangular roof piece to wrong side of roof (with door) along 4″ edges; check to make sure angle fits house sides (if not, adjust accordingly). Paint house and ladder brown; paint rungs honey yellow; paint remaining pieces hunter green. When dry, center roof on house; glue door to house side below roof opening; glue large window centered on opposite house side. Glue small window centered on back house end (end closest to swinging door). Glue rungs to ladder, spacing evenly. Set house and ladder aside.

To shape ark, spread sheet of aluminum foil on work surface; fill bowl with water. Following manufacturer's directions, knead wood pulp dough until pliable, working on foil to facilitate easy cleanup. Shape, following *Ark Sculpting Diagram* and pattern; scoop out center and cut out notch on one side for ladder as shown. Position house in ark with small window facing stern (rounded end); smooth dough over bottom of house so there are no demarcation lines. Shave and smooth gunwales of ark with hatpin. When satisfied, let dry thoroughly for 24–36 hours. When dry, rub lightly with fine sandpaper. Paint interior brown; paint exterior and gunwales honey yellow.

All Figures : To shape Noah and the animals, spread sheet of aluminum foil on work surface; fill bowl with water. Following manufacturer's directions, knead wood pulp dough until pliable, working on foil to facilitate easy cleanup. Shape following *Sculpting Diagrams* and directions below; use fingers, hatpins, and toothpicks to mold, curve, and smooth dough to just the right shape. If necessary, sand away any rough edges by rubbing lightly with fine sandpaper.

Noah : Shape pointed cylinder for body; shape one small bell-shaped cylinder for each sleeve; roll two small balls for hands and press into ends of sleeves. Press tops of arms to shoulders of body. Roll ball for head; indent for eyes; apply small piece for nose. Flatten piece of dough into a circle and drape over head for hair and beard; cut out opening for face; incise moustache. Press head on body. Let dry. Paint face and hands flesh, hair reddish brown, and clothing dark brown; paint in black eyes. Glue dowel to body over right hand.

Birds : Shape two birds following diagrams; when satisfied, position on roof near front of ark, angling birds slightly toward one another. Press firmly to roof, forming an indentation in the dough, then remove and let dry. Paint birds blue with yellow beaks.

Glue each to roof along indented area on body.

Giraffes : Shape two giraffes following diagrams, making one slightly shorter than the other. Add small triangular pieces of dough for ears; use toothpicks to incise front and back legs. Add small worm of dough to rear for tail. Let dry. Paint body yellow with reddish-brown spots; paint in white eyes with black pupils.

Elephants : Shape male elephant following complete diagrams; add worm of clay to rear for tail; remove excess dough between front and back legs; indent dough for toes. Flatten dough and shape for ears, then press to head. For female elephant, sculpt same as for male, except lift head upward slightly and bend trunk up as shown in partial diagram. Let dry. Paint elephants gray with red mouths, white eyes and toenails, and black pupils. For male, paint white tusk on each side of head.

Lions : Shape two lions following diagrams; add small rounded bits of dough for ears; add worm of dough to rear for tail and press against one side of body. Use hatpin to incise toes and sculpt face. For male lion, add dough around neck for mane; incise hair lines with pin. Let dry. Paint lions yellow with dark brown eyes, nose, mouth, toes, and tip of tail. On male lion, paint mane brown.

BIRDS

ADAM AND EVE STAND-UP

NOTE: Before beginning, read General Directions for Transferring Designs on page 14.

Skill Level: Intermediate.

Materials: Watercolor paper: 50 lb. bond, 400 lb. bond. 1/4″ basswood, one 1 × 22″ sheet. White glue. Aluminum foil. Pencil. Scissors or mat knife. 6″ half-round bastard file or medium-weight sandpaper. Tack cloth. Gold paint. Watercolor paints: colors shown in photograph. Rapidograph pen. Taube's Damar Picture Varnish. Straight pins. Gouge.

Directions: This ornament is constructed in the same way as the Decorated Wafers on page 40. Trace the pattern and transfer two outlines to each weight of watercolor paper. Transfer the entire design to one of the heavyweight paper pieces. Use scissors or mat knife to carefully cut out each of the four pieces. Glue layers together following directions for Wafer ornaments, omitting hanging loop. Weight and dry as directed.

While ornament is drying, cut one 4 1/2 × 1″ piece of basswood. Using pencil and ruler, draw a lengthwise line along center of one side of basswood. Using gouge, make a groove 1/8″ wide and 1/8″ deep along marked line. Sand carefully and dust with tack cloth.

After ornament is dry, carefully sand cut edges until quite smooth, using file or sandpaper; edges should look like one piece of paper. Dust carefully. Using watercolor paints and following pattern and photograph, paint design on front; allow paint to dry thoroughly before working an adjacent color unless you are blending colors. After basic design has been painted, add gold highlights and other small details following pattern and photograph. When satisfied with painted design, glue bottom edge of ornament to groove made in basswood base. Let dry thoroughly. Paint back, sides, and base of ornament gold. Coat with varnish in a well-ventilated room.

The Lichtstock

Christmas and candlelight are almost synonymous. No other Christmas ornament has defied the barriers of time, place, religion, and nationality the way the candle has. It truly belongs to everyone, and at no time is this more evident than at Christmas.

Who has not been mesmerized by the flickering dance of a candle flame? The reason for its universal appeal is not hard to find. Candlelight doesn't simply illuminate, it transforms, creating an aura of mystery, serenity, and reflection—qualities, incidentally, that accord perfectly with Christmas.

The mysterious way candles have of transforming their surroundings probably accounts for the enduring appeal of the Lichtstock, which is, without a doubt, the oddest-looking member of the great family of decorated trees. At first glance, a Lichtstock resembles a bric-a-brac shelf in the shape of a tepee. In fact, the original Lichtstock was not a tree at all but an open wooden pyramid with shelves attached. The shelves sometimes supported gifts or small ornaments, but above all they were designed to hold candles, for the Lichtstock—a name that means light-stick in German—was really an elaborate candlestand.

To anyone whose idea of Christmas includes a richly decorated floor-to-ceiling evergreen, the Lichtstock may seem a sparse and awkward contrivance. But stand a Lichtstock in a darkened room, light the candles on each shelf, and it becomes a gleaming pyramid of light that conveys the spirit of Christmas in a way no other decorated tree quite matches.

In seventeenth-century Germany, where the Lichtstock first became popular, candles were not only the primary source of illumination but also a powerful religious symbol, as they had been for centuries. Anyone who has read the Bible or listened to a sermon knows that Jesus Christ is called the Light of the World, and it is not difficult to think of other ways that Christians have used the image of light to express religious ideas. One of the most fascinating images of candlelight occurs in an old French poem called "Durmar the Frenchman." In the course of his wanderings, Durmar comes upon a tree that is full of lighted candles, some upright, some upside down, and has at its top a figure of the Christ Child. Astonished, Durmar asks the meaning of the tree. "The lit tree is humanity," his companion replies. "The upright lights are the good men, the reversed lights the bad men, and the Child is the Savior." This and similar stories express what many have felt intuitively: that candlelight is miraculous. A glowing Lichtstock is the expression of that feeling.

Yet candles are only one of the decorations on a Lichtstock. In Germany it was customary to wind evergreen branches around each leg of the pyramid and to grace the apex with a star or pinecone, while small gifts, wooden figures, and pastries filled the shelves. These decorations were retained when the Lichtstock spread to other countries, whose people added their own distinctive touches. In Herefordshire, a county in western England on the Welsh border, the Lichtstock was decorated with gilded evergreens, apples, and nuts. At Christmas and New Year's there, it was customary for children to carry small Lichtstocks about the village and offer them as gifts.

The most flamboyant-looking Lichtstocks were made in Italy, where they were known as *ceppi,* or logs, which may indicate that the Lichtstock replaced the custom of decorating and burning a Yule Log at Christmas. Florentine *ceppi* were made of laths or cane and stood 1 1/2 to 3 feet high. Their moss-covered cardboard shelves and coils of red paper spiraling up each leg gave these *ceppi* the appearance of Christmas confections. Family members placed small gifts on the upper shelves, reserving the lowest shelf for a manger scene.

Despite its singular appearance, seemingly unrelated to any other decorated tree, the Lichtstock is one of the great-grandparents of the modern Christmas tree. In the seventeenth century, German families often stood a glowing Lichtstock beside an undecorated fir tree on the day before Christmas. (In some regions of Germany, notably Bavaria, this custom persisted into the nineteenth century.) In time, however, the two trees were blended: the Lichtstock's candles were attached to the boughs of the evergreen, and the star was taken from its apex and placed at the very top of the fir, which became the center of the Christmas celebration.

THE LICHTSTOCK

NOTE: Before beginning, read Note on Use of Candles on page 13.

Skill Level: Intermediate.

Materials: 3/4″ plywood, 19″ square. Compass. Jig saw. Sandpaper, medium and fine. Wooden dowel, 7/8″ diameter, 30″ long. Wood glue. Flathead nail, 2″ long. Hammer. Green paint. Paintbrush. Three wire wreath forms: 8″ diameter, 12″ diameter, 18″ diameter. Evergreen branches. Lightweight wire. Red satin ribbon: 1″ wide, 5 1/2 yards; 1/2″ wide, 2 yards. Scissors. Measuring tape. Small red apples. Pastries and cookies.

Directions: On plywood, draw two concentric circles, 18″ and 7/8″ in diameter. Cut out larger circle using jig saw; drill a hole in smaller circle before inserting jig saw blade for cutting. Sand cut edges with medium, then fine sandpaper. Insert dowel into center hole: sand if necessary until dowel fits snugly. Drive nail into center top of dowel, allowing nail head to extend 5/8″ above dowel. Paint entire armature green, making sure dowel can be removed easily from hole; let dry thoroughly. Cover dowel, base, and each wreath form with greens, wiring securely and making sure branches are all facing in the same direction.

Cut twelve 14″ lengths of 1″

ribbon. For smallest wreath, tie four ribbons around branches and wire form at north, south, east, and west positions. Drop wreath over dowel and tie ends of each ribbon to nail at top so wreath is suspended. Tie four ribbons around 12″ wreath form as described above. Remove dowel from base and insert through center of 12″ wreath, then back into base. Tie ribbons from second wreath to first wreath, matching north, south, east, and west positions; make sure ribbons are tied evenly so wreath hangs straight. Attach third wreath in same

manner as second wreath, tying ribbons to second wreath. Secure dowel to base using wood glue.

To decorate tree, tie remaining length of 1″ ribbon into a bow; attach to top to cover nail. Cut 1/2″ ribbon into 6″ lengths; tie into bows around branches. If desired, make candleholders as directed on page 34, and add to Lichtstock. Otherwise, wire candles to Lichtstock. Arrange apples between lowest wreath and dowel. Attach small pastries (see page 35) and cookies to the branches with wire.

STAR CANDLEHOLDER

NOTE: Before beginning, read General Directions for Ceramics on page 14 for additional materials and directions.

Skill Level: Intermediate.

Materials: Pre-wedged porcelain clay that fires to cone o6. Two 3/8″ lattice strips. Wooden dowel, 5/8″ diameter. Transparent overglaze. Two gold beads. Dark green fine wire.

Directions: Trace star pattern onto sturdy cardboard and cut out. Roll slab of clay between 3/8″ lattice strips. Use pattern to cut star shape from clay; bore wiring holes in star using trimming needle and following open circles on pattern for position. Allow star to sit until slightly firm, then push end of wooden dowel into center of star until clay yields. At the same time, push each point of star up slightly toward dowel; see photograph. You now have a small pocket in the center to hold a candle; pocket will protrude about 1/4″ on wrong side. Allow to dry leather hard, then bisque-fire to cone o6. Paint outside of candleholder with transparent overglaze; do not allow overglaze to clog wiring holes. Fire to required cone.

To make hanging loop, follow *Wiring Diagram* to thread wire through star, beads, and back through star, twisting wires tightly underneath as shown.

WIRING DIAGRAM

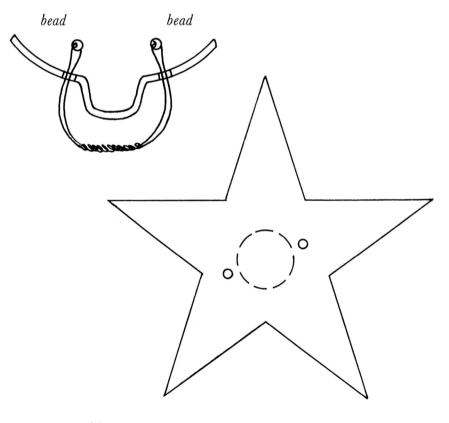

bead   *bead*

34

MINIATURE PINWHEEL PASTRY

SKILL LEVEL: Intermediate.

RECIPES:

PASTRY DOUGH
1 pkg. active dry yeast
1/4 cup warm water
1/4 cup sugar
3 1/2 cups all-purpose flour
1 egg
1/4 cup milk
1/2 tsp. vanilla
1/2 tsp. salt
1/4 tsp. ground cardamom (optional)
1/2 tbsp. sweet butter
1/2 lb. sweet butter (2 sticks)

1. Pour warm water in a small bowl; sprinkle dry yeast on water; sprinkle one tsp. sugar onto yeast mixture and let stand for a few minutes. Stir mixture until the yeast is dissolved, then place the yeast mixture in an unlighted oven until it doubles in bulk.

2. Measure 2 1/2 cups flour into a large mixing bowl. Make a "well" in the center of the mound and add the egg, milk, vanilla, salt, cardamom, tbsp. sweet butter, and the remaining sugar. Stir to form a soft dough, then shape into a ball and knead on floured surface for 10 minutes. The dough will appear smooth and shiny. Sprinkle the dough with flour, wrap in aluminum foil, and refrigerate for 45 minutes.

3. Meanwhile, place the two sticks of butter, side by side, on a sheet of floured waxed paper; place a second floured sheet over the sticks. Roll the butter with a rolling pin to form a rectangle approximately 6 × 8" and about 1/4" thick. Place in refrigerator for 1/2 hour.

4. Roll out pastry dough on floured surface until it measures 7 × 14" and 1/8" thick.

5. Remove butter from refrigerator and cut in half so each half measures approximately 4 × 6"; place one rectangle on the center of the rolled dough. Fold one side of rolled dough over butter. Place the second rectangle of butter on top of the folded side. Cover that rectangle of butter with remaining side of rolled dough. Seal top and bottom edges by pinching closed. Flour and wrap in foil, then refrigerate for 1/2 hour.

6. With the narrow side facing you, roll the chilled dough into a 6 × 14" rectangle. Fold in half. Flour and wrap in foil, then refrigerate for 1/2 hour.

7. Roll the chilled dough to form another 6 × 14" rectangle: fold both narrow ends in to meet the center, then fold in half again. Flour and wrap in foil, then refrigerate for 1/2 hour.

8. Roll the chilled dough and repeat procedure #7. Flour and wrap in foil, then refrigerate for 3 hours.

FILLING
1/4 cup granulated sugar
ground cinnamon
egg white from 1 egg
1 tsp. water
coarsely crushed walnuts

1. Preheat oven to 375° F.

2. Roll out the pastry dough into a 9 × 16" rectangle on floured surface.

3. Mix egg with water and brush on surface of dough.

4. Combine the sugar and cinnamon and sprinkle on rolled-out dough. Also sprinkle walnuts on dough.

5. Place a sheet of waxed paper over rolled dough and filling; using rolling pin, gently roll the filling into the dough.

6. Peel off the waxed paper and roll the dough into a long log.

7. Cut off little rings about 3/8" thick, and place on greased and floured cookie sheets.

8. Bake for 10 minutes at 375° F., then turn oven down to 300° F. and bake for 15 more minutes.

9. Cool on rack.

The Christbaum

Among the things travelers bring or send back home are their impressions of foreign lands, and these have often included some precise and fascinating observations of Christmas customs abroad. Countless English and American visitors to Germany in the nineteenth century wrote letters filled with wonder and delight at the Christmas trees and ornaments they were seeing for the first time. Although similar firsthand accounts from earlier periods are rare, we owe our earliest glimpse of a decorated tree standing in a parlor to a traveler who visited Strasbourg in 1605. "At Christmas time," he recorded in his diary, "fir trees are set up in the rooms at Strasbourg and hung with roses cut from paper of many colors, apples, wafers, spangle-gold and sugar. It is customary to surround it with a square frame. . . ."

This tree was called the Christbaum (literally, "Christ-tree"), and it takes us back to an age when religion played a much greater role in everyday life than it does today. For that reason, the meaning of many of the decorations our traveler described may be unclear. The apples, of course, refer to the fall of Adam and Eve, and the Communion wafers to man's salvation through Jesus Christ. But what about the paper roses? In the seventeenth century, the rose was considered a symbol of the Virgin Mary as well as the emblem of love and beauty that it still is today. But like so many Christmas customs, the origin of the rose as an ornament is found in popular legend, in this case, one that dates from the tenth century. It was said that on the night Christ was born, flowers and trees miraculously blossomed the world over. This legend gave rise to the practice of decorating the Christmas tree with paper roses and also to the custom of cutting a branch from a cherry or other flowering tree, rooting it indoors during the winter, and forcing it to bloom in time for Christmas.

In every age, people have added their own fancies to Christmas trees, and the Christbaum was no exception. Embellishments such as Christ-bundles—little packets crammed with candy, sugarplums, and cakes—reflected the sheer joy people of the time felt at Christmas. (The word *Christ-bundle,* incidentally, reflects the popular belief of the period that all gifts came from the Christ Child; Santa Claus didn't really become part of Christmas until the nineteenth century.) In time, pastries began to replace Communion wafers as decorations. They were made in two colors: white dough was shaped into flowers, bells, stars, angels, and hearts, while brown dough was used to make figures of men and animals.

Today we automatically picture a Christmas tree standing on the floor, but this was not always the custom. The tree our traveler saw apparently stood on a table and was surrounded by a fence of some kind, which perhaps enclosed a small landscape, a tradition that has continued down to the present. The Christbaum also appeared in other forms in Germany, Austria, and Alsace. A number of seventeenth-century drawings show it hanging from the rafters of a cluttered room, in some instances with its stem sharpened to a point from which an apple is suspended. In parts of Germany and Austria it was customary to form a Christbaum using only the tip of an evergreen, which was hung upside down from the rafters and decorated with bits of red paper, gilded nuts, and apples.

The Christbaum was so popular in German cities and towns in the seventeenth century that laws were passed to prevent the excessive cutting of fir trees. The Alsatian village of Ammerschweier, for example, forbade anyone to have for Christmas "a bush of more than eight shoe lengths," which translates into a tree approximately four to five feet high.

The Catholic Church viewed the Christbaum with disdain, as it did many popular Christmas customs of the time. In the 1640s, the Strasbourg theologian Johann Conrad Dannahauer uttered what amounted to an ecclesiastical "Bah, humbug" on the subject. "Among the other trifles," he wrote, "which are set up during Christmastime instead of God's word, is the Christmas tree or fir tree, which is put up at home and decorated with dolls and sugar." He would not be the last churchman whose condemnation of the decorated tree fell on deaf ears.

PAPER ROSE

Skill Level: Elementary.

Materials: Tissue paper, red or white. Florist's wire. Green florist's tape. Scissors. Ruler. Pencil.

Directions: Cut one 3″ and one 4″ square of tissue paper. Crumple 3″ square into a ball; place ball at one corner of 4″ square. Fold opposite corner of 4″ square toward ball, sandwiching ball between layers of tissue and forming a triangle. Next, fold other two corners of triangle toward ball, then roll and twist folded paper to resemble a tight bud, with crumpled ball at base of bud. Wrap floral wire around base of bud, securing paper.

Trace pattern for rose petal seven times onto tissue paper; cut out seven petals. Add petals all around bud, one at a time, and with straight bottom edges even with base of bud; wrap with wire to secure. When last petal has been added, make a 1 3/4″ stem with length of doubled wire. Wrap base of flower with florist's tape, covering wiring; continue down to cover stem. Pull tape taut while wrapping; wrap tightly for a firm, straight stem. Twist stem around tree branch.

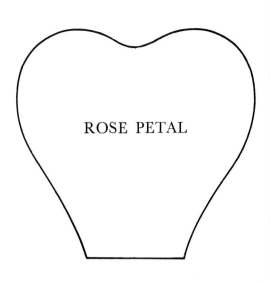

ROSE PETAL

HERBAL MOTIFS

DECORATED WAFERS

NOTE: Before beginning, read General Directions for Transferring Designs on page 14.

Skill Level: Intermediate.

Materials: Watercolor paper: 50 lb. bond, 400 lb. bond. White glue. Aluminum foil. Pencil. Compass. Scissors or mat knife. 6″ half-round bastard file or medium-weight sandpaper. Tack cloth. Silver cord for hanger. Gold paint. Watercolor paints: colors shown in photographs. Rapidograph pen. Taube's Damar Picture Varnish. Straight pins.

Directions: Each ornament requires two layers of 50 lb. bond paper (lightweight) sandwiched between two layers of 400 lb. bond paper (heavyweight). For each ornament, use a compass to draw two 2 1/8″ circles on each weight of paper. Trace the desired pattern, and transfer to one heavyweight paper circle for wafer front. Use scissors or mat knife to cut out all circles.

Paint wrong side of wafer front with layer of white glue; paint one side of one lightweight circle with glue and press to wafer front with edges even and glued sides facing.

Starting in center, press together gently outward to the edges; wipe away excess glue as you press it out. Cut a 4 1/2″ length of silver cord and glue ends to lightweight circle to form hanging loop, making sure loop will be at top of design. Glue second lightweight circle to first one in manner described above, securing hanging loop. Next, glue heavyweight circle to lightweight one, again as described. Place glued wafer between two layers of aluminum foil, then weight down with heavy books, weights, or other heavy objects. Let dry for 24 hours or longer to prevent buckling.

Using file or sandpaper, carefully sand edges of glued wafer until quite smooth; edge of wafer should look like one piece of paper. Dust carefully with tack cloth, then paint back and sides gold up to marked circle on wafer front. Following patterns and photograph and using watercolor paints, paint design on front, allowing paint to dry thoroughly before working an adjacent color unless you are blending colors. Add highlights and other small details with rapidograph pen after basic design has been painted, following pattern and photograph.

When satisfied with painted design, coat with varnish in a well-ventilated room. Hang ornaments from cork or bulletin board to dry, using straight pins to separate them and prevent wafers from sticking together.

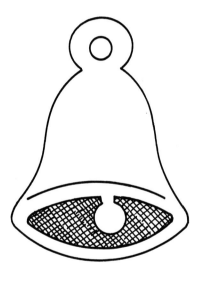

"WHITE DOUGH" BELL AND PRETZEL

NOTE: Before beginning, read General Directions for Ceramics on page 14 for additional materials and directions.

Skill Level: Intermediate.

Materials: Pre-wedged porcelain clay that fires to cone 06. Two 1/4″ lattice strips. Tracing paper (for bell). Loop. Transparent overglaze. Satin ribbon for hanging.

Directions: For bell, trace outline onto sturdy cardboard; trace entire design on tracing paper. Cut out both patterns. Roll slab of clay between 1/4″ lattice strips. Use cardboard pattern to cut out shape from clay. Place tracing paper pattern over clay bell and transfer inner lines of design to clay by pricking through the paper with a trimming needle. Use trimming needle to cut out inner top circle entirely. Use loop and trimming needle to gently carve out shaded area to 1/8″ depth. Use trimming needle to trace smooth line above carved area.

For pretzel, trace entire pattern onto cardboard. Cut out, including inner sections. Roll slab of clay between 1/4″ lattice strips. Use pattern to cut pretzel shape from clay; use trimming needle and loop to remove entire inner sections of design.

Allow ornaments to dry leather hard, then bisque-fire to cone 06. Dip in transparent overglaze, clean hanging loop of bell and center bottom hole of pretzel, and hang on rod in kiln. Fire to required cone. Thread satin ribbon through loop of bell and bottom hole of pretzel; tie for hanging loop.

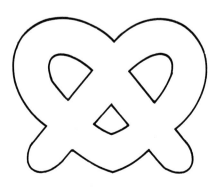

42

"BROWN DOUGH" ASS AND SHEPHERD

NOTE: Before beginning, read General Directions for Ceramics on page 14 for additional materials and directions.

Skill Level: Elementary.

Materials: Terra-cotta clay with grog that fires to cones 06–10. Two 1/4″ lattice strips. Porcelain slip. Paintbrush. Transparent overglaze. Ribbon for hanging.

Directions: Trace ass and shepherd patterns onto sturdy cardboard and cut out. Roll slab of terra-cotta clay between 1/4″ lattice strips. Use patterns to cut shapes from clay; bore a hanging hole in each ornament using trimming needle and following open circle on pattern for position. Allow to dry leather hard, then paint outer edges and between other decorative lines with porcelain slip. Bisque-fire to required cone. Apply a transparent overglaze and fire to required cone.

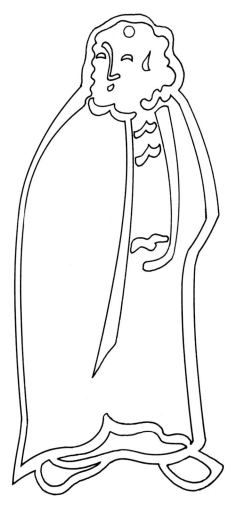

43

The English Tree

In December, 1848, an engraving appeared in the *Illustrated London News* that some say singlehandedly caused the English to adopt the decorated tree as a Christmas custom. It showed Queen Victoria and her husband, Prince Albert, flanking a richly decorated evergreen, while their five children gazed at this marvel in wonder and delight. The picture caused an immediate sensation in Britain, as it did two years later when *Godey's Lady's Book,* an immensely popular magazine published in Philadelphia, reproduced it (with some changes) for American readers. The British public responded heartily to the warm, human portrayal of the Royal Family and were as taken with the royal Christmas tree as Victoria and Albert's children were.

The tree had been Albert's idea. He had been born in 1819 in Coburg, then a small town on the border between Saxony and Bavaria in south central Germany, a region rich in Christmas customs. In 1840 he married Victoria, who was his first cousin, and who had ascended to the throne only three years before. Albert was ill at ease in English society at first, and perhaps out of a nostalgic remembrance of Christmas past in Germany, he put up a Christmas tree in Windsor Castle in 1841, the year after his first son, Albert Edward (later Edward VII), was born. At least that is the impression he gave in a letter written to his father in December, 1841, in which he expressed sadness at being separated from his parents at Christmas. He consoled himself, however, by reflecting on Christmas in Windsor Castle. "Today I have two children of my own to make gifts to," he wrote, "who, they know not why, are full of happy wonder at the German Christmas tree and its radiant candles."

Albert's was probably the most delectable decorated tree in history. Hanging from its branches were a multitude of elegant trays, baskets, and receptacles in the shape of gazebos and pavilions filled with the richest, most expensive sweets money could buy. Suspended from colorful ribbons were ornately decorated cakes, gilt gingerbread in various shapes, and glacé fruits. Perhaps five feet high, the tree stood on a table covered with white damask and was surrounded at its base by gifts for the children and piles of more sweets too heavy to hang on the tree. Among the gifts were bonbonnières in the shape of small cottages, knights on horseback, soldiers, dolls, and pull toys, each with the recipient's name affixed to it. At the top of the splendid tree stood an angel with outstretched wings holding a wreath in each hand.

Albert's was not the first decorated tree erected in England. In 1516, Henry VIII presented a Christmas pageant at court, which had as its centerpiece an evergreen made of gold. Queen Charlotte, wife of George III, who like Albert came from a German royal family, had a decorated tree in her lodge at Windsor Castle in 1800. It stood in a tub of dirt on the floor and was decorated with paper cones filled with almonds and raisins, fruits, toys, and wax candles.

But the custom of decorating an evergreen at Christmas had never really caught on among ordinary Englishmen, who regarded the Christmas tree as an essentially German custom. Albert's tree changed all that. He publicized the custom by giving decorated trees to schools and barracks, and the popularity of the Royal Family did the rest. Only two years after the famous engraving appeared, potted evergreens—which the English, in tribute to the Royal Family, called Royal Trees—

were being sold in Covent Garden Market each December.

Not every Englishman had the royal kitchen at his disposal to make treats as elaborate as those Albert provided for his children. Nonetheless, animal-shaped cookies dusted with sugar and paper cones and woven baskets filled with fruits, nuts, and candy became popular decorations overnight. In the days before Christmas, English kitchens were often filled with the aroma of homemade toffee and peppermint drops, which were frequently hidden inside hollow pieces of imitation fruit to be hung on the tree as decorations.

The ordinary Englishman's tree was a grand sight. Bright red bows of ribbon contrasted smartly with the deep green boughs, Union Jacks stood at attention on the tips of the branches, and little men whose heads came off to reveal a trove of sweets within peeked out from the needles. The tree was also laden with an astonishing variety of paper ornaments, which were made at home in the weeks before Christmas. A favorite design was a guitar cut out of cardboard, covered with bright green satin, and given a set of snappy-looking strings made of yellow thread. Cardboard Turkish slippers embellished with white silk, colored satin, or velvet added an exotic touch to the tree. Cones made of bright-green, satiny paper were adorned with scarlet tassels, filled with sweets, and hung on the branches, along with paper drums and paper cylinders that had satin sacks filled with scent sewn on each end.

Probably the favorite ornament, though (at least among the little girls), was the Lucky Shoe. It was made of cardboard and filled with sweets and scented wadding. One Lucky Shoe also had a ring hidden inside it. After the Christmas dinner, the paper ornaments were often raffled off as party favors, and the girl who got the Lucky Shoe containing the ring was supposed to be the first to get married.

There were also porcelain roses hung on the sturdier branches, Delft hearts and stars, small wreaths of flowers, and garlands of Christmas cards, which were a Victorian innovation.

But it was the toys that gave the English tree its wonderfully cluttered appearance. Victorian London was filled with toy stores and bazaars, especially in the vicinity of Ludgate Hill, which was the home of London's penny toy trade. At Christmas it was not uncommon to see shoppers with sacks moving from vendor to vendor buying these metal miniatures, which were hung on the tree. They were made in the shape of delivery vans, donkeys, dogs, soldiers, horses, and a hundred other objects. Ratchet-driven toys were a special favorite for boys. They were wound up with a key, and when placed on the floor, rolled along on concealed wheels. They were often made in the shape of animals, and the toymakers tried to make the movement look as real as possible by building the toy so the legs of the animal moved. No tree was complete without steam train miniatures and pull toys, especially horses.

All kinds of dolls were likely to be found on and under the tree. Some had porcelain heads and leather bodies, others were made of wax. Porcelain dolls were frequently seen because they were inexpensive, as were white-bisque dolls smartly turned out in soldiers' uniforms or fancy gowns.

Gifts that made especially pretty ornaments were pincushions. They were usually made at home and in a variety of shapes—boats, stars, fish—and a good deal of care was lavished on them. Most were made of brightly colored plush or silk and were trimmed with ribbons or gold cord.

Because this tree had been popularized in England by a German prince, the famous Victorian novelist Charles Dickens dubbed it "the new German toy." In December, 1850, he gave the readers of *Household Words*, a magazine he edited, a glowing description of a tree set up in an English parlor. "There were witches standing in enchanted rings of pasteboard, to tell fortunes; there were teetotums, humming tops, needle cases, pen wipers, smelling bottles, conversation cards, bouquet holders, real fruit made artificially dazzling with gold leaf; imitation apples, pears, and walnuts, crammed with surprises; in short, as a pretty child before me delightedly whispered to another pretty child, her bosom friend, 'there was everything and more.' " The English decorated tree was truly a cornucopia of gifts and a child's paradise: when else have gifts ever grown on trees so abundantly?

PULL-TOY HORSES

NOTE: Before beginning, read General Directions for Transferring Designs on page 14 and General Directions for Woodworking on page 15.

Skill Level: Intermediate to Advanced.

Materials: (for two horses) Basswood: 1/8″ square × 22″ stripping; 1/4″ square × 22″ stripping; one 1/4 × 1 1/2 × 22″ sheet. Dowels, 24″ long: 3/16″ diameter; 3/4″ diameter; 7/8″ diameter. #10 coping saw. Gouge. Sandpaper, medium and fine. Tack cloth. Oaktag. Scissors. Acrylic paints: white, black, red, blue, purple, green, orange. Metallic gold paint. Paintbrushes. Gold metallic thread or red rattail. Red/gold soutache braid, 1/8″ wide, or gold braid with fringe, 1/4″ wide. Star sequins. Black or white thread or crochet cotton. Wood glue. Polyurethane spray. Fine gold wire.

Directions: For each horse, trace patterns for head, tail, and base. Transfer to 1/4″ basswood sheet. Cut out, using coping saw. Following *Wood Cutting Chart,* cut additional body pieces for each horse from stripping and dowels. On base, use gouge to carve two grooves for the axles in between dash lines on pattern; make grooves about 1/8″ deep. Sand all pieces with medium, then fine sandpaper; dust with tack cloth.

For body, follow *Measured Body Diagram* to angle back end and sand front edges. Sand away about 1/8″ at bottom to make it flat. When satisfied with body, glue legs to flat bottom, 1/8″ away from front and back edges; angle legs outward slightly so legs are about 1/4″ apart at the hoofs. Glue head to center top of body, about 1/8″ away from front edge. Paint horse desired color. Paint tail in a contrasting color; glue to angled back portion of body, even with top.

Paint axles and axle ends the same color; paint wheels in a contrasting color, adding decorative lines in another color if desired. Glue one axle, centered, between two wheels. Glue axle ends, centered, to outside of wheels. Paint base desired color; add a floral design in a variety of colors if desired. When dry, glue axles to base along gouged grooves.

Glue handles to each side of handle shaft 1/4″ away from one end; paint desired color.

Glue shaft inside notched section of base at an angle as shown in photograph. Glue horse, centered, to base. Spray ornament several times with polyurethane spray to achieve a glossy finish. Let dry.

For harness, use gold metallic thread or rattail; wrap and glue around muzzle and head as shown in photograph. For reins, cut 5″ length of red/gold soutache or gold braid with fringe; glue ends to upper body just behind head, allowing reins to loop around body front. Cut strands of thread or crochet cotton, and glue to head for a thick mane and forelock.

Complete half-pattern for desired blanket. Use pattern to cut one blanket from oaktag; transfer design to oaktag and paint with acrylics and gold metallic paint. Glue sequin star in position on each side; let dry. Drape and glue blanket over horse's body, covering ends of reins. Secure to branch with gold wire.

WOOD CUTTING CHART
(For One Horse)

WOOD	NAME OF PIECE	NUMBER OF PIECES	LENGTH
1/8″ square	handle	2	1/4″
1/4″ square	handle shaft	1	2 1/4″
1/4″ square	leg	4	1 3/4″
3/16″ dowel	axle	2	1 1/2″
3/16″ dowel	axle end	4	1/8″
3/4″ dowel	wheel	4	1/4″
7/8″ dowel	body	1	3″

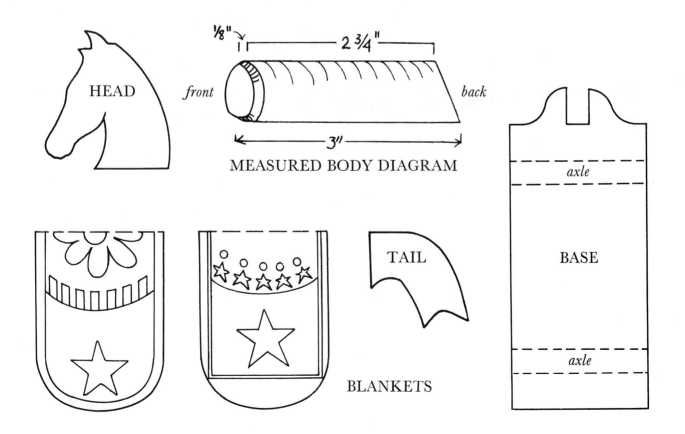

HEAD

1/8"

2 3/4"

front

back

3"

MEASURED BODY DIAGRAM

TAIL

BASE

axle

axle

BLANKETS

HEAD

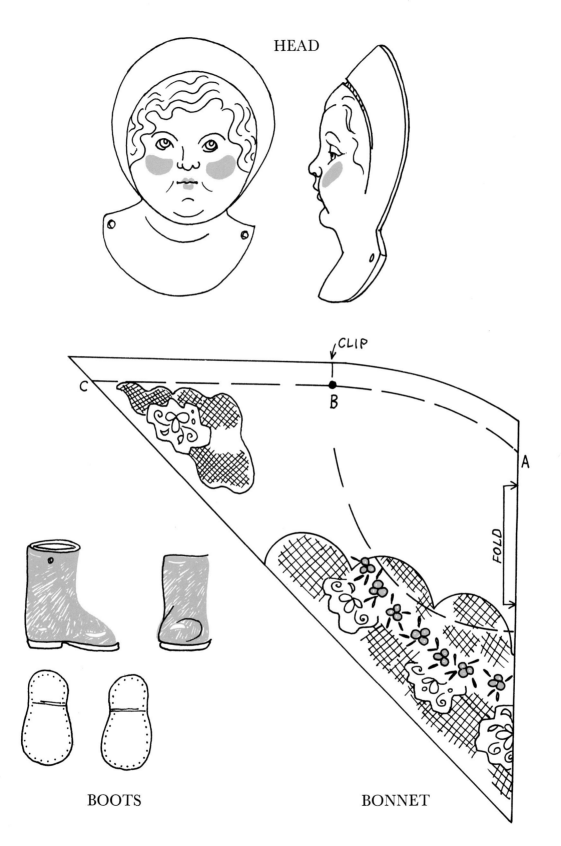

CLIP

C

B

A

FOLD

BOOTS

BONNET

50

ANTIQUE PORCELAIN DOLL

NOTE: Before beginning, read General Directions for Ceramics on page 14 and General Directions for Sewing on page 15 for additional materials and directions.

Skill Level: Advanced.

Materials: *For Ceramic Parts:* Pre-wedged porcelain clay that fires to cone o6. Ceramichrome One-Stroke Translucent Underglaze, rose pink. Ceramichrome OK Dinnerware Glaze, clear gloss. Loop. Stilts. Acrylic paints: black, blue. *For Body and Clothes:* Muslin 36″ wide, 1/4 yard. Fiberfill. Three matching antique handkerchiefs with netting, lace, or appliqué worked in corners and around edges. Antique scalloped lace trim 1″ wide, 1/4 yard. Pink satin ribbon 1/8″ wide, 1/4 yard. Pink seed beads. Green embroidery floss. Embroidery, sewing, and beading needles. Matching thread. White glue.

Directions: *Ceramic Body Parts:* Following actual-size *Sculpting Diagrams,* form a head, two hands, and two boots from porcelain clay. Work slowly and carefully, wetting trimming needle if necessary to scribe clean shapes and smooth curves. Shape head first, making fat cheeks and rounded chin and forehead. Use loop to carve indentations for eyes. Shape tiny nose and nostrils as shown. Incise wavy hair with trimming needle.

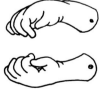

HANDS

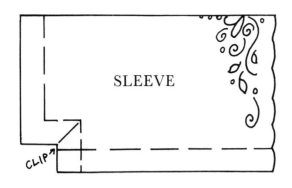

SLEEVE

CLIP

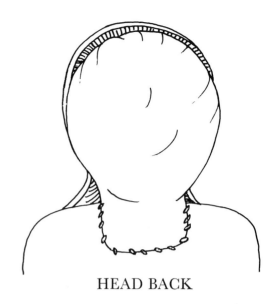

HEAD BACK

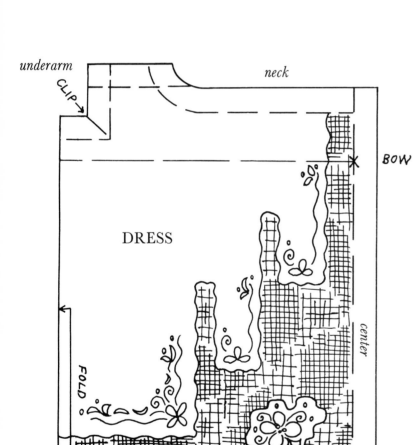

underarm

CLIP

neck

DRESS

BOW

center

FOLD

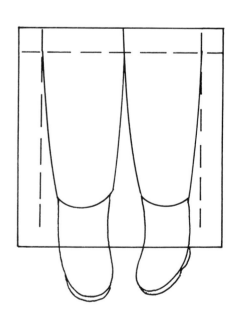

BODY ASSEMBLY
DIAGRAM

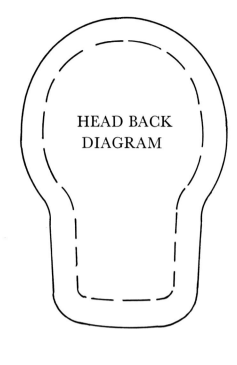

HEAD BACK DIAGRAM

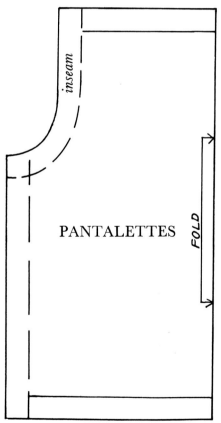

inseam

PANTALETTES

FOLD

Shape neck and chest, boring a hole in each corner with trimming needle. Allow to dry leather hard while working on other pieces, then carefully place layer of fiberfill over the face. Turn head over and place fiberfill and face in the palm of your hand. Using trimming needle and loop, remove excess clay from back of head, leaving a rounded cavity about 1/2" deep. Work very slowly, being careful not to cut through to the sculpted side and not to press or flatten the sculpted area.

Fashion one left and one right hand and forearm using trimming needle to carefully form each finger; curve hands as shown. Use trimming needle to bore hole through each forearm in position indicated on diagram. Shape left and right boots as shown, making small heel and pressing point of needle into clay around edge of sole to simulate nails. Use trimming needle to bore hole through upper portion of each boot in position indicated on diagram.

Allow all pieces to become bone dry. Using pink underglaze, paint pink lips and cheeks. Paint boots pink, leaving soles and 1/16" along bottom edges white. Propping pieces on stilts, bisque-fire underglaze to required cone. Coat with overglaze. Flatten two pieces of wet clay into thick pancakes. Wipe away glaze on ends of boots, arms, and legs, then insert ends in pancake; be sure glaze does not touch pancakes or clog bored holes. Fire to required cone. Using acrylics,

paint in black eyes; rim eyes delicately with blue.

To Make Body: Cut the following pieces from muslin: two 2 3/4 × 3" torso pieces, two 2 × 2 1/4" arms, and two 2 1/2 × 3" legs. Pin torso pieces together; stitch 3" edges together, forming a tube. Stitch long edges of legs together, forming two tubes; turn to right side. At one end of each tube fold edges 1/4" to wrong side and baste. With seam centered at back, insert top of boot into basted edge of leg; attach by sewing through bored holes and wrapping thread around boots and fabric. Stuff legs with fiberfill until medium firm; baste across top edges. Following _Body Assembly Diagram,_ insert legs inside torso with feet in correct position, and stitch in place. Turn torso to right side; stuff with fiberfill as for legs. Turn raw edges 1/4" inside and slip-stitch opening closed. Make arms as for legs; stuff with fiberfill and finish as for body. Tack arms to shoulders with hands in correct position. Place ceramic head over body; glue, then tack in place through bored holes. Cut one head back from muslin, using pattern. Press all raw edges to wrong side. Fill cavity of head with fiberfill, then glue pressed edges of head back to edges of ceramic piece. When you reach the fabric body, slip-stitch edges of head back to body; see _Head Back Diagram._

To Make Clothes: For pantalettes, use pattern to cut two pieces from muslin. Pin legs together along inseam and stitch, making two separate legs; turn one leg to right side, insert inside other leg, and stitch crotch seam. Make 1/4" hem along waist and bottom edges. Place on doll.

For dress, use patterns to cut two dress pieces and two sleeves from two handkerchiefs. Position decorative corners of handkerchiefs at center front of dress following pattern; position finished edges of handkerchiefs along hems of sleeves and dress. Stitch dress pieces together along center front and center back. Stitch straight shoulder seams; clip seam allowances at underarms. Stitch underarm seams of sleeves; baste around each sleeve cap. Ease sleeves into armholes and stitch. Fold raw neck edges to wrong side and slip-stitch in place, clipping as necessary. Hand-baste around dress on long dash line. Place dress on doll; pull basting gently, gathering dress to fit doll around chest; tie off basting. Tie pink satin ribbon into a bow; tack to center front of dress at X.

For bonnet, fold remaining handkerchief in half diagonally with corner design along fold; position pattern at edge of fabric along fold as indicated and cut out one bonnet. Sew clusters of pink seed beads to fabric all around bonnet; embroider tiny straight-stitch stems using two strands of green floss in needle. Hand-baste on long dash line between B's; clip seam allowance where indicated. Fold bonnet in half with wrong sides facing; stitch seam

allowance between A and B. Turn to right side; continue stitching seam allowance between B and C. Place on doll; pull basting, gathering bonnet to fit doll's head; tie off basting. Fold portion of bonnet between B and C up toward crown; tack in place. Fold other point of bonnet over as shown in photograph; tack in place. Nestle doll in branches.

CERAMIC ORNAMENTS: FLORAL HEART AND STAR; ROSE HEART

NOTE: Before beginning, read General Directions for Ceramics on page 14 for additional materials and directions.

Skill Level: Elementary.

Materials: For All: Pre-wedged porcelain clay that fires to cone 06. Two 1/8" lattice strips. Transparent overglaze. Satin ribbons for hanging. For Floral Heart and Star Ornaments: Underglaze: Ceramichrome Tranz One Stroke translucent.

Directions: Floral Heart and Star Ornaments: Trace heart and star patterns onto sturdy cardboard and cut out. Roll slab of clay between 1/8" lattice strips. Use patterns to cut heart and star shapes from clay; bore hanging holes in ornaments using trimming needle and following

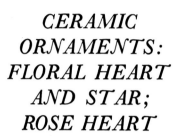

FLORAL HEART
AND STAR

ROSE HEART

open circles on patterns for position. Allow to dry leather hard, then bisque-fire to required cone. Using fine paintbrush and desired underglaze, paint design on one side of each ornament following pattern as a general guide. Bisque-fire to required cone. Dip in overglaze, clean hanging hole, and hang on rod in kiln. Fire to required cone.

Rose Heart Ornament: Trace heart pattern onto sturdy cardboard and cut out. Roll slab of clay between 1/8″ lattice strips. Use pattern to cut heart shape from clay. Roll a small piece of clay into a worm shape; attach ends to make a circle. Add a drop of water at the center top of heart, and attach circle for hanging loop following pattern. Crosshatch small section in center front of heart; set heart aside.

To make rose, tear off small sections of clay one at a time, each no larger than the pad of your thumb. Following *Diagram A,* flatten and roll clay like a scroll for center of flower; push down on the top gently to make edges look natural. Continue adding petals to the first scroll as shown in *Diagram B,* pinching and shaping them until you are satisfied that they look like petals. Keep clay moist while working. As you hold the rose in shaping, an extra clay "handle" will form at the bottom. When satisfied with rose, use knife to trim excess off bottom. Crosshatch bottom, add a drop of water to crosshatched center of heart, and press rose in place following *Diagram C.* Allow ornament to become bone dry, then bisque-fire to cone specified on package. Apply transparent overglaze and fire to specified cone.

DIAGRAM A   DIAGRAM B   DIAGRAM C

PORCELAIN EGG

NOTE: Before beginning, read General Directions for Ceramics on page 14 for additional materials and directions. These instructions are for egg at extreme right in photograph; other eggs pictured are variations.

Skill Level: Advanced.

Materials: Pre-wedged porcelain clay that fires to cone o6. Chocolate-egg mold, about 2 3/4 × 3 1/2″ (available in gourmet cooking stores). Aluminum foil. Trowel. Cake decorator's presser, heart stamp. Lattice strips: two 1/4″ and two 1/8″. Loop. Kemper Tools #K45 Klay Gun, ribbon disc. Ceramichrome OK Dinnerware Glaze, clear gloss.

Directions: Line egg mold

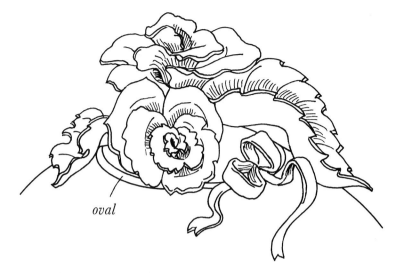

oval

SCULPTING DIAGRAM

DECORATIVE STRIP

with aluminum foil to facilitate easy removal. Roll out clay between 1/4″ lattice strips and gently press into mold. When clay has hardened slightly, remove the two halves from the mold; gently peel away the aluminum foil. Crosshatch edges of each half, apply slip, then gently press halves together. Roll a worm of clay; press on seam and gently trowel into the seam.

Roll another worm of clay and press on center top of egg, forming an oval about 1 1/2 × 2″; crosshatch center of oval. Using cake decorator's presser, stamp hearts into clay between edge of oval and seam; stamp hearts in even, staggered rows so edges of hearts touch.

Roll 1/2 × 10 1/2″ length of clay between 1/8″ lattice strips. Crosshatch one side of strip and troweled seam around egg. Apply slip and gently press clay strip around egg at seam line; remove any excess so there is no overlap. Following *Decorative Strip Diagram*, sculpt a curvilinear, leafy design all around egg, using loop and trimming needle. Roll thick worm of clay into a circle for hanging loop. Add slip to decorative strip at rounded end of egg; press one edge of loop into slip to secure.

To make rose, tear off small sections of clay one at a time, each no larger than the pad of your thumb. Flatten and roll clay like a scroll for center of rose; push down gently on top to make edges look natural. Following *Sculpting Diagrams*, continue adding petals to first scroll, pinching and shaping them until you are satisfied that they look like petals. Keep clay moist while working. As you hold rose in shaping, an extra clay "handle" will form at the bottom. When satisfied with rose, use knife to trim excess off bottom. Crosshatch bottom, add drop of slip to crosshatched oval, and press rose in place on egg, following diagrams for position. Make second rose in same manner.

For leaf, press clay between thumb and index finger until clay is quite thin; trim edges and score veins with trimming needle, then squeeze and push clay until it resembles leaf in diagrams. Attach to egg as for rose; make and attach second leaf in same manner.

For ribbon, use clay gun and ribbon disc to shape about 10″ length of ribbon. Cut and shape into bow with streamers, following diagrams; gently crosshatch one side of ribbon and egg. Add slip, then press ribbon in place.

It is important that there be at least two openings to the center cavity to allow air and gases to escape so the form does not explode in the kiln. Allow egg to dry leather hard, then perforate each end with trimming needle. Allow egg to become bone dry. Bisque-fire to cone 06. Paint with overglaze on top and sides, leaving base free of glaze. Fire to required cone. Display under tree.

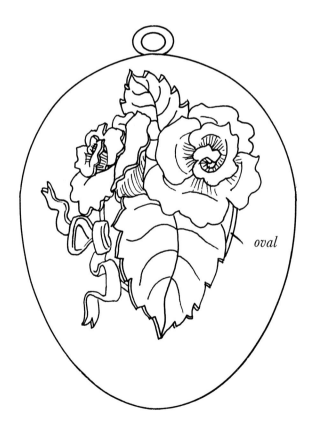

oval

SCULPTING DIAGRAM

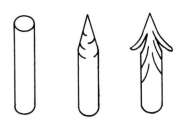

TREE DIAGRAM

ENGINE BASE

COAL CAR

COACH

CABOOSE

CAB

STEAM TRAIN AND TUNNEL

NOTE: Before beginning, read General Directions for Woodworking on page 15 for additional materials and directions.

Skill Level: Intermediate.

Materials: Basswood: 1/16″ square × 24″ stripping; 1/8 × 3/8 × 22″ sheet; 1/8 × 1 1/2 × 22″ sheet; 1/4″ square × 22″ stripping; 1/4 × 3/8 × 22″ sheet. Dowels, 1/16″ and 1/4″ in diameter. White glue. X-acto knife. Acrylic paints: black, red, blue, kelly green, olive green, yellow, white, brown. Metallic gold paint. Seed beads: red, black, white. Gold pearl cotton. Gold me-tallic thread. Oaktag. Wire. Palette knife.

Directions: *Preparation:* For each car and base, cut pieces from basswood, dowels, or stripping using coping saw or X-acto knife. Sand each piece with medium, then fine sand-paper; dust carefully with tack cloth. Paint and assemble, fol-lowing individual directions.

For wheels, cut sixteen 1/8″-wide sections of 1/4″-diameter dowel. Sand; dust; paint black. After cars have been assembled, glue wheels to each base so 1/8″ of dowel di-ameter extends below base. En-gine: From 1/8 × 3/8″ bass-wood, cut one 3/8″ square top. From 1/4″ square stripping, cut one 3/8″ cab and one 3/4″ base; angle front of base fol-

59

lowing pattern. For smokestack, cut 1/8" length of 1/16"-diameter dowel. For motor, cut 3/8" length of 1/4"-diameter dowel; sand one end into rounded shape. From 1/16" stripping, cut two 3/8" lengths. Sand; dust; paint top black, stripping and smokestack gold, and remaining pieces olive green.

Glue cab vertically to base with back edges flush. Center and glue top over cab. Glue motor to base with rounded end in front; glue wheels to base; glue stripping to wheels at an angle. Glue white seed bead to front of motor, and glue smokestack atop motor near front. Paint gold stripe around bottom edge of top piece and on each side of motor. Paint windows and flowers on each side of cab following pattern. Paint yellow wavy stripes along top edge of base and bottom edge of motor on each side.

Coal Car: From 1/8 × 3/8" basswood, cut one 5/8" base. From 1/4 × 3/8" basswood, cut 1/2" bin; angle one edge of bin following pattern. Sand; dust; paint blue. Decorate sides of bin with gold borders and red and yellow flowers following pattern. Glue bin to base with edges flush; glue wheels to base. Glue 10 black seed beads to top of bin for coal.

Coach: From 1/8 × 3/8" basswood, cut two 3/4" pieces for top and bottom. From 1/4"-square stripping, cut 5/8" coach. Sand; dust; paint top and bottom black and coach kelly green. Paint black win-dows on coach following pattern; decorate with floral motif. Center and glue coach between top and bottom; glue wheels to base. Paint gold stripe around bottom edge of top piece.

Caboose: From 1/8 × 3/8" basswood, cut two 3/4" pieces for top and bottom. From 1/4 × 3/8" basswood, cut 1/2" coach. From 1/16" stripping, cut one 3/8" length and two 1/4" lengths for back railing. Sand; dust; paint top and bottom black, coach red, and stripping gold. Following pattern, paint black windows and blue, yellow, and black floral motif on each side of coach. With edges flush at one end, glue coach between top and bottom; glue wheels to base beneath coach section. Paint a gold stripe around bottom edge of top piece. Glue two red seed beads to back end of top. For back railing, glue two 1/4" pieces of 1/16" stripping vertically to base; glue 3/8" piece across vertical pieces.

For tree, cut 1" length of 1/4" dowel; shape top to a point using X-acto knife and sandpaper. Following *Tree Diagram,* use X-acto knife to shave branches. Carefully slice X-acto upward against dowel, starting with uppermost branches, and working downward until you have exposed a strip at bottom for trunk. Paint trunk brown and tree kelly green. Glue tree to roof of caboose; wrap pearl cotton around tree and glue ends to caboose top.

To connect cars, cut 3" length of gold metallic thread; glue to bases of each car, spacing cars evenly, starting with engine, then coal car, coach, and caboose. Set aside.

Base and Tunnel: From 1/8 × 1 1/2" basswood, cut a 4 1/4" piece for base. Sand; dust. Mix black and white paint for gray, and paint top and side edges of base. Paint other side kelly green. From 1/16" stripping, cut two 4" lengths for rails; cut twenty-three 5/8" lengths for ties. Paint black. Center and glue ties to base so they are evenly spaced and parallel to short edges. Glue rails over ties, spacing rails about 1/8" apart. Glue train to rails with caboose at one edge.

For tunnel, cut 3/4 × 5 1/2" strip of oaktag. Paint one side gray; paint other side as if to simulate large gray bricks. Cut 4" length of wire; fold in half. Starting at fold, twist 1 1/2" and shape into a hook; insert ends of wire through center of oaktag from right (brick) side; separate wires and run around sides and back up to hook; wrap ends around hook and clip off excess. Bend oaktag lengthwise into a U with brick side outward and hook at top; glue to each side of base in front of engine, holding securely until glue dries. To simulate snow, use palette knife to mound white acrylic paint over top of tunnel (covering wire), on sides of tracks, and on tops of cars and tree; let dry thoroughly.

BED WITH EMBROIDERED COVERLET

NOTE: Before beginning, read General Directions for Transferring Designs on page 14 and General Directions for Embroidery on page 16.

Skill Level: Advanced.

Materials: Four ready-made turned wooden posts, 5 1/2″ long. Basswood: 1/8″ square × 22″ stripping; 1/8 × 1/2 × 22″ sheet; 1/8 × 2 × 22″ sheet. Small coping saw. X-acto knife. Medium and fine sandpaper. Tack cloth. Stain. Brush for stain. White glue. Oaktag. Muslin, 45″ wide, 1/4 yard. Calico fabric, 1 × 24″ with selvage along 24″ edge. Miniature scalloped lace trim 3/8″ wide, 1/3 yard. Two flat gold sequins. Six-strand embroidery floss, one skein each of the following: ivory, baby yellow, maize, brown, baby blue, medium blue, royal blue, pink, rose, red, spring green, kelly green, purple. Embroidery needles. Small embroidery hoop. Graphite paper. White thread. Batting. Ribbon for hanging.

Directions: *Bed:* Trace pattern for headboard and transfer to 1/8 × 2″ basswood using graphite paper; cut out with coping saw. Incise flower design using tip of X-acto knife. Cut two 4 1/4″ side rails and one 2 1/2″ foot rail from 1/8 × 1/2″ basswood; sand one long side edge of each piece to round

corners. Cut two 4 1/4″ supports from 1/8″-square stripping. Sand all pieces lightly with medium, then fine sandpaper; dust with tack cloth; stain all pieces.

With curved, sanded edges of side rails upward, glue supports to side rails with bottom edges even, forming a shelf. Cut a 2 5/8 × 4 1/4″ piece of oaktag; glue oaktag between side rails and onto shelf formed by supports. Cut two 2 5/8 × 4 1/4″

layers of batting; glue evenly to oaktag. Cut a 3 1/2 × 10″ piece of muslin; press one short and both long edges 1/4″ to wrong side. Wrap lengthwise around padding and oaktag; slip-stitch pressed short edge over raw edge at bottom (unpadded side). Glue long pressed edges of muslin to inner side rails and to supports on underside. Glue one post to ends of each side rail so top sanded edges of rails are 1″ above base of posts.

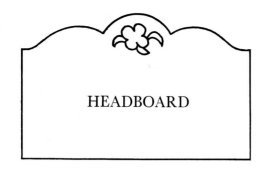

HEADBOARD

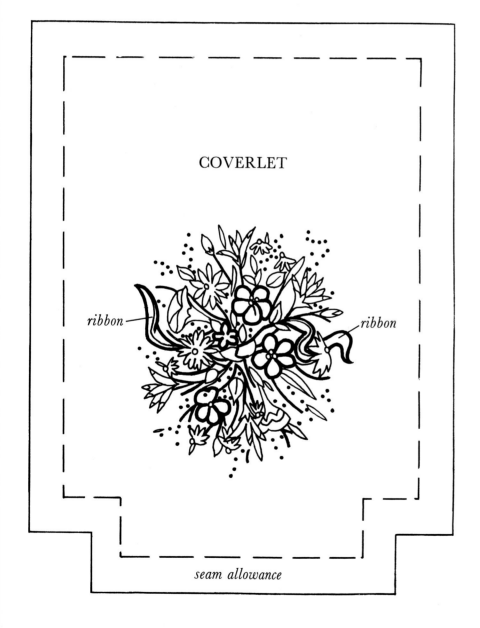

COVERLET

ribbon

ribbon

seam allowance

Glue headboard between one pair of posts and glue footboard between the other pair so bottom edges are even with side rails. Cut calico into one 6″ and two 9″ strips. Machine-baste along each raw edge; pull basting to gather each ruffle to fit foot and side rails. Glue raw edges in place, adjusting gathers evenly. Cut one 2 1/2″ and two 4 1/4″ lengths of lace trim; glue over raw edges of ruffles. Glue one gold sequin to each post at foot of bed.

Coverlet: Trace coverlet pattern, including embroidery design. Cut 8 × 9″ piece of muslin. Center pattern over right side of fabric, leaving equal margins around all edges; using graphite paper, transfer embroidery design and outline to fabric.

Using two strands of floss in needle, embroider design as follows: Work ribbon first in baby blue satin stitch, highlighted with medium blue, and outlined in royal blue (heavy line). Work background stems indicated by medium-weight lines in outline stitch, interspersing brown and greens. Next, work flowers in long and short stitch, working flowers outlined by heavy lines in shades of pink, rose, and red; work other flowers in ivory, purple, or shades of yellow. Work centers of red flowers in spring green French knots; work centers of all other flowers in maize French knots. Work leaves in spring green satin stitch; outline-stitch around each leaf with kelly green. Finally, work all black dots in medium blue French knots.

When embroidery is completed, steam-press gently on padded surface with embroidered surface face down. Carefully cut out along outer line. Use coverlet top to cut lining from muslin. With right sides facing, sew lining to top, leaving opening for turning at top edge. Clip corners; turn to right side; fold raw edges inside and slip-stitch opening closed. Press.

For pillow, cut one 4 × 4 3/8″ piece from muslin. Fold in half, matching 4 3/8″ edges; stitch three sides together, leaving opening for turning. Clip corners; turn to right side; stuff with batting until plump. Fold raw edges inside and slip-stitch opening closed. Slip-stitch pillow to coverlet at sides and top, having folded edge near center of quilt. Place coverlet on bed; pin in place securely. Tie ribbon around one bedpost; knot ends to make loop for hanging.

STRAWBERRY CONTAINING TINY DOLL

NOTE: Before beginning, read General Directions for Transferring Designs on page 14, and General Directions for Embroidery on page 16.

Skill Level: Intermediate.

Materials: Scraps of muslin and white cotton. Olive green felt. Seed beads: white, yellow, green. Fiberfill. Velcro closure strip, 1/4 × 2″. Six-strand embroidery floss: light brown, blue, pink, spring green. Acrylic paints: red, white, yellow. Sewing and embroidery needles. Matching thread. White glue. Compass.

Directions: (for one strawberry and one doll) Trace pattern and use to cut ten strawberry sec-

tions from muslin. Pin two sections together, right sides facing, and sew one side from point to point; pin and sew three more sections to the first two, attaching each along one side to make one group of five. Make second group of five in the same manner. With right sides facing, pin two groups together around edges; sew together, leaving opening for stuffing. Turn to right side; stuff lightly with fiberfill. Fold raw edges of opening inside, then slip-stitch opening closed. To secure open edges of strawberry (to hold the surprise), sew Velcro closure strip to right side of one edge and wrong side of the other edge.

Mix red and white acrylic paints with water to achieve a strawberry-colored wash; test on scrap fabric until satisfied with shade. Paint outside of strawberry with wash, shading color from light at one end (base) to

dark at other end (top). Let dry; then sew white seed beads randomly over entire berry.

Use pattern to cut one strawberry top from olive green felt; tack center to top of strawberry, then tack leaves to sides, twisting and shaping them as you stitch for a natural effect.

For fabric flower, cut four 2 1/2″-diameter circles from white fabric. Hand-baste 1/8″ away from raw edge of each circle; pull basting to gather edges together tightly and tie off. Hold gathered edges of each petal between thumb and forefinger, then wrap thread around raw edges of all four, holding petals securely together. On right side, sew three yellow seed beads in center of gathered petals; sew green seed beads around yellow ones. Use pattern to cut one flower calyx from olive green felt. Cut 10″ length of green embroidery floss; thread all six strands through needle. Knot one end and run needle through center of calyx, securing knot on one side. Glue knot side of calyx over gathered raw edges of flower. Run needle threaded with same floss through top of strawberry; knot end securely inside. Knot center portion of strand, making 2″ hanging loop.

Fill center of strawberry with small candies, or make doll as follows: Trace and transfer entire pattern for doll to right side of white fabric; transfer outline and edges of face and hands to fabric for back. Mix red, yellow, and white acrylics with water for a pale flesh wash; paint head and

hands on each piece. Using two strands of embroidery floss in needle, embroider blue eyes in straight stitch and pink mouth in straight stitch. Embroider hair around face and entire back of head with light brown French knots. Embroider all dots on dress with pink French knots; embroider all lines on dress with green straight stitch. Draw 4 × 1 1/2″ skirt on white fabric; cut out all pieces.

With right sides facing, sew doll front and back together to inner edges of hands; do not sew across edge indicated by dash lines. Clip where indicated and along all curves. Turn to right side; stuff with fiberfill. Delineate edges of

hands with running stitch through fabric and fiberfill. Sew a tiny hem along one long edge of skirt; sew short edges together with right sides facing. Baste around raw edge and pull to gather. With right side of skirt inside and seam at back, insert doll, head first, into skirt, matching dash-line edge of doll to raw gathered edge of skirt. Whip-stitch together all around, adjusting gathers. Pull skirt down, exposing doll; tack bottom edges of skirt together if desired. Make hanging loop with white thread and attach one end to top of doll's head; attach other end inside strawberry. Insert doll into strawberry and close Velcro fastener.

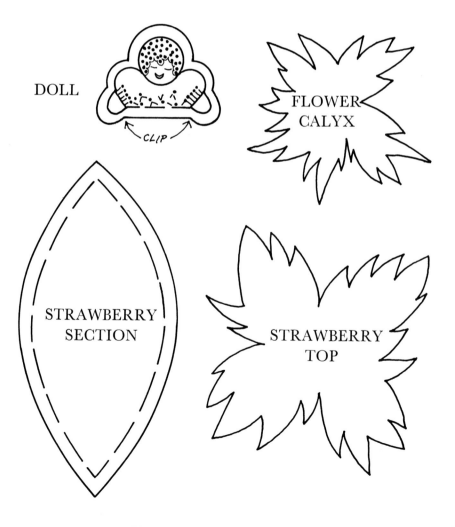

DOLL

CLIP

FLOWER CALYX

STRAWBERRY SECTION

STRAWBERRY TOP

PULL-TOY LAMB (*see next page for instructions*)

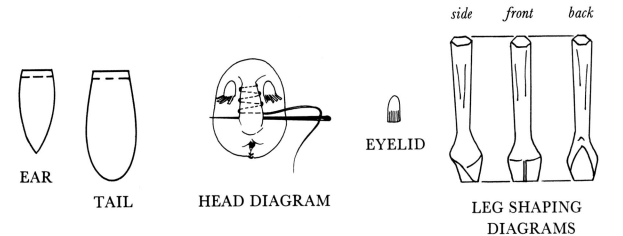

EAR

TAIL

HEAD DIAGRAM

EYELID

side   front   back

LEG SHAPING
DIAGRAMS

65

PULL-TOY LAMB

Skill Level: Intermediate.

Materials: Large scrap of ivory-colored fleece fabric. White muslin. Compass. Scissors. Sewing needle. White thread. Fiberfill. Knitting needle. Acrylic paints: black, blue, red, green. Paintbrush. Dry rouge. Green pearl cotton. Basswood dowels, 3/8″ and 1/2″ diameter. 1/4″ basswood, 2 1/4 × 22″ sheet. Coping saw. X-acto knife. Sandpaper. Tack cloth. White glue. Red wooden bead, 5/8″ diameter. Gold filigree jewelry finding for bell. Fine gold wire.

Directions: Use compass to mark a 2 1/2″-diameter circle on muslin; cut out. Fill center of circle with fiberfill, then gather raw edges together and wrap thread around fabric, forming a 1″-diameter muslin ball; ball should be stuffed to medium firmness. Holding the ball with the top facing you, shape face as follows: Pinch fabric and some fiberfill down the center and stitch from side to side following *Head Diagram* to form snout. To make mouth, use knitting needle to push in fabric and fiberfill about 1/4″ below end of snout; pinch any folds that may form below mouth, and tack. Then run needle through the indentation and behind head several times, pulling thread tight to hold the mouth's shape. Use pattern to cut two eyelids from muslin; remove threads along straight edge to form eyelashes. Glue

eyelids to either side of snout, slightly cupped so they have dimension. Paint inside of mouth red; paint eyes blue. Rub rouge on cheeks, then set head aside.

For body, cut 4 × 7″ rectangle from fleece. Fold in half with right sides facing and raw edges even, matching 4″ edges. Sew long edges and one short edge together, rounding off corners. Turn to right side; hand-baste around top edge 1/4″ from raw edges. Stuff with fiberfill. Insert head into opening and pull basting, gathering body around head just above eyes and just below mouth. Push raw edges of body carefully inside, then slip-stitch body securely to head. Cut two ears and a tail from fleece. Tack ears to body just above head; tack tail to rear.

To make legs, cut four 1 1/2″ lengths from 3/8″ dowel. Following actual-size *Leg Shaping Diagrams*, use X-acto knife to shape legs by gradually shaving off wood. When satisfied with legs, dig X-acto knife deeply in center front of each to form cloven hoof. Paint hoofs black. Wrap and glue scraps of fleece around upper 3/4″ of each leg. Glue legs firmly to bottom of lamb. Tie pearl cotton collar in a bow around lamb's neck; tack gold filigree bell just below bow.

Use coping saw to cut one 2 1/4 × 4 3/4″ base from basswood. From 1/2″ dowel cut four wheels, each 1/8″ thick. Sand all rough edges; dust with tack cloth. Paint base green and wheels red. Glue wheels to sides

of base, 1/4″ away from front and back edges. Glue lamb's feet to base so lamb is centered. Cut 3 1/2″ length of pearl cotton. Tie one end around red bead; glue bead to front of base at one corner. Glue other end of pearl cotton to center front of base. Secure to branch with wire.

PEDDLER DOLL

NOTE: Before beginning, read General Directions for Sewing on page 15.

Skill Level: Advanced.

Materials: Cotton fabric, 45″ wide, 1/4 yard each: mauve and unbleached muslin; scraps of tan, blue/green print, and other assorted solids and prints. Scraps of white eyelet trim, 1/2″ wide. Fiberfill. Acrylic paints: white, red, yellow, blue, steel gray. Brown felt-tipped fine-line marking pen. Gray fake fur with at least a 2″ nap. Brown felt. Oven-bake modeling compound. Fine wire. Black medium-weight wire for glasses. Wire cutters. Straight pins. Toothpicks. 3/16″-square wooden beads in beige and various colors. Rapidograph pen. Three gold jewelry findings, 1/4″ diameter. Seed beads: pink, blue, white. White bugle beads. Blue satin ribbon 1/4″ wide, 1/8 yard. Gold pearl cotton. Thread to match fabrics. 1/16″ basswood, 2 × 22″ sheet. Glue. X-acto knife. Paintbrush.

Directions: Cut 6″-diameter circle from muslin for head.

FACE SCULPTING DIAGRAMS

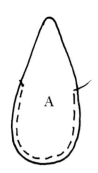

A Stitch around bottom to gather slightly

E Stitch nose into shape

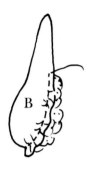

B Stuff bulbous part

F Stitch to form bridge of nose

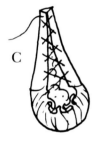

C Lightly stuff upper part. Fold under raw edges. Gently sew closed with cross-stitches

G Pinch and sew to make eyelids

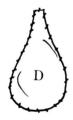

D Slip-stitch onto face

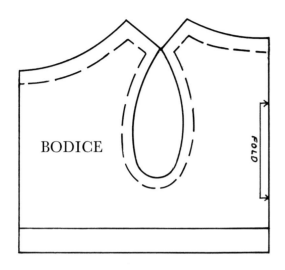

BODICE

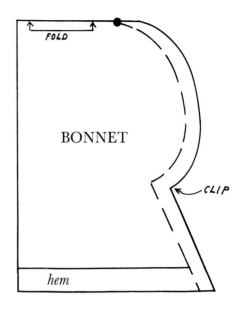

BONNET

FOLD

FOLD

hem

CLIP

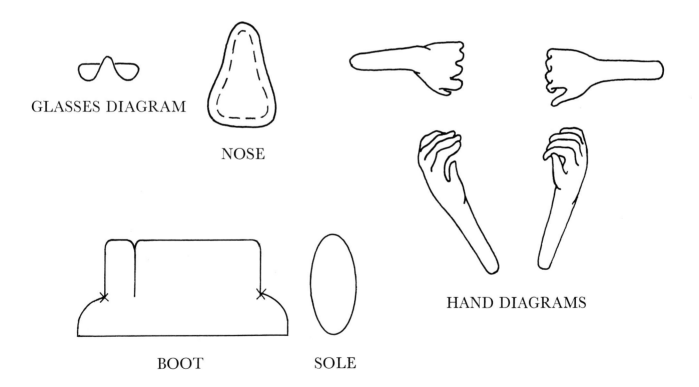

GLASSES DIAGRAM

NOSE

HAND DIAGRAMS

BOOT

SOLE

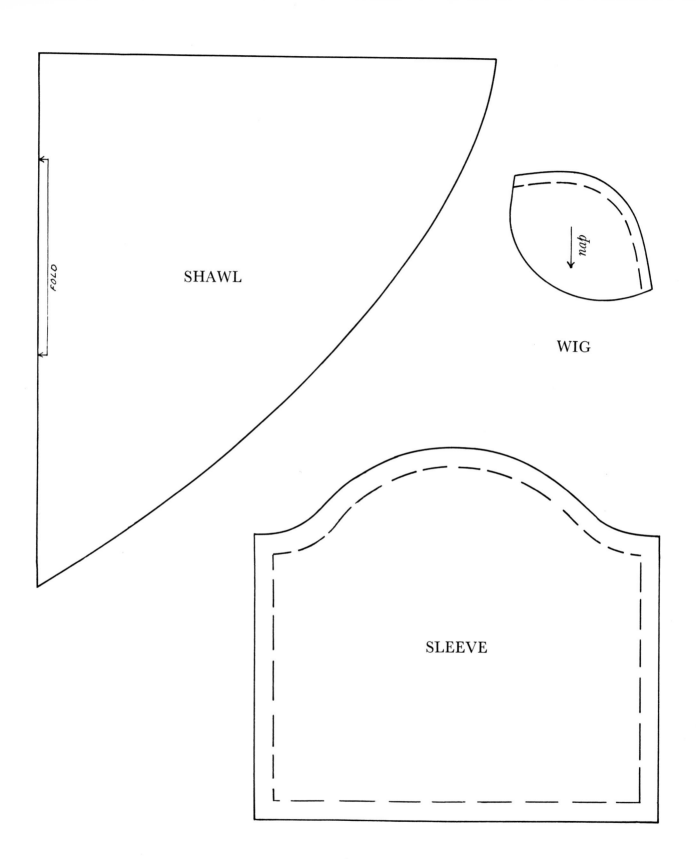

SHAWL

FOLD

WIG

nap

SLEEVE

BEAD DOLL FACE

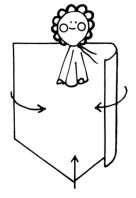

BABY DOLL DIAGRAM

BEAD DOLL DIAGRAM

TRAY DIAGRAM

Hand-baste around muslin circle, 1″ from raw edges, using strong thread. Gently gather perimeter of circle, forming a pouch. Fill center of pouch with fiberfill until stuffed to medium firmness. Pull basting tight and adjust gathers of muslin ball, concentrating major gathers on one side of ball, which will later be the back of the head. Tie off thread. Using pencil, lightly mark positions for eyes, nose, and mouth on upper half of ball; features will appear to be high.

Trace all patterns. Use pattern to cut out nose from muslin. Gather bottom of nose and stuff gathered portion with fiberfill (*see Diagrams A* and

B). Then lightly stuff upper portion of nose. Secure fiberfill inside nose with cross-stitches (*see Diagram C*); do not pull thread too tightly or close the opening. Slip-stitch nose to marked position on face (*see Diagram D*).

To form nostrils and bulbous portion of nose, work each side separately as follows: Pinch top and bottom of one side of nose between thumb and index finger. Secure pinched area with four or five tiny stitches; start stitches from underneath nose where nostril will be, running needle through fiberfill toward side of nose. Stitch toward middle of nose and be sure to pull thread

tightly between stitches (*see Diagram E*).

To form bridge of nose, start thread from inside of one nostril and come out on one side of bridge. Run stitches behind bridge, from one side to the other, until length of bridge is pinched and folded (*see Diagram F*).

To form eyelids, pinch a narrow fold of fabric and fiberfill over each eye. Curve fold slightly, running tiny stitches through it to secure fabric and fiberfill (*see Diagram G*). To set off lower part of eye, make small running stitches through fabric and fiberfill, pulling stitches taut to form indentations. Some laugh or squint

71

wrinkles will form as you do so—these are desired.

To form cheeks, work each side separately. Pinch a fold on an angle from nose toward jaw. Secure fold with running stitches, ending just below mouth line. Continue stitches, curving upward, to form bottom of cheek, while simultaneously working fiberfill upward to puff cheek (*see Diagram F*). Try to make second cheek same size as the first. Delineate mouth with tiny running stitches curving upward. Make a double chin with tiny running stitches.

Make flesh-colored acrylic paint using a dab of white paint in cup of water; add small dabs of red and yellow, and mix well. Paint entire head evenly except for eyes. While face is still wet, dilute dab of red paint in another cup of water and apply to cheeks; let red bleed into fabric. If bleeding does not occur, dip brush in plain water and brush around cheeks, blending red into flesh evenly. Paint lips red; do not allow bleeding. Paint eyeballs white. When dry, mix blue paint with steel gray and dab on for irises. Use rapidograph pen to add pupils. Paint white or light gray highlight at top left corner of each iris. Outline eyes with brown felt-tipped fine-line marking pen; test it on scrap fabric to make sure brown doesn't bleed.

When satisfied with head, set aside and prepare wig. Using pattern, cut one pattern and one reverse pattern from gray fake fur, both with nap going in one direction (follow arrow); do not cut through the fur, but do cut through the backing, separating the strands carefully. Sew wig pieces together along marked seamline, which becomes the "part." Glue wig to head, then brush hair toward the back and make a bun; stitch bun lightly in place with matching thread.

Cut 3 1/2 × 4″ body, two 2 3/4 × 2″ legs, and two 1 1/4 × 2 1/2″ arms from muslin. Fold body in half, matching 3 1/2″ edges; sew across long edge and one short edge, making a pouch. Turn to right side; baste around top edge. Stuff pouch with fiberfill until very firm. Insert head into opening and pull basting, enclosing fiberfill and raw edges of head. Tie off. Push raw edges of body inside, and slip-stitch head firmly to body. Fold each leg in half matching 2 3/4″ edges; sew across long edge and one short edge, making a pouch. Turn to right side and stuff firmly with fiberfill. Fold raw edges inside and slip-stitch closed. Sew each leg firmly to bottom of body. For arms, fold each in half, matching 2 1/2″ edges; sew as for legs. Turn to right side and stuff lightly with fiberfill. Fold raw edges 1/4″ inside. Following actual-size *Hand Diagrams*, fashion two hands (one left and one right) from modeling compound; use pins and toothpicks to carefully form each finger, curving hands as shown. Bake, following package directions, then paint flesh, using acrylic paint left over from face. Insert wrist of each hand inside fabric arm; wrap thread around fabric and wrist, securing hand to arm. Attach arms securely to body with thumbs pointing upward.

Cut two boots and two soles from brown felt; clip boot along marked line for tongue. Fold boots in half, matching toes, and sew toes to marked X. Turn boots to right side. Position sole at bottom of boot and whip-stitch in place. Stuff toes lightly with fiberfill, then slip each boot on a foot, centering tongue; secure with a small stitch at base of tongue.

Cut two sleeves and one 4 1/2 × 4″ apron from muslin. Cut one bodice, one 10 × 4″ skirt, and one 1 1/4 × 6″ bonnet facing from mauve fabric. Cut one bonnet from tan fabric. Cut shawl from blue/green print fabric.

Stitch side edges of sleeves; machine-baste around sleeve cap and wrist edges. Pull basting, gathering each end of sleeve. Slip one sleeve onto each arm. Turn raw edges of sleeve cap 1/4″ to wrong side and slip-stitch to body, positioning seam under the arm and adjusting gathers evenly. When sleeve cap is in place, pull basting tightly around wrist, hiding wound thread; tie off, pushing raw edges inside sleeve.

Fold skirt in half with right sides facing, matching 4″ edges; stitch seam. Fold hem under 1/4″, then again 1/4″, and slip-stitch in place. Machine-baste around opposite edge. Slip skirt on peddler with seam at center back and basted edge at waist;

pull basting, gathering skirt to fit snugly. Tie off; slip-stitch skirt to waist. For apron, press both 4″ edges and one 4 1/2″ edge under 1/4″ twice and slip-stitch in place. Machine-baste across raw edge; pull basting, gathering top of apron to 2″ width. Center apron on peddler's front; slip-stitch raw edge to waist.

For bodice, clip raw edges at armholes and neck, and press 1/4″ to wrong side; press bottom edge and one edge of bodice front to wrong side. Stitch shoulder seams. Slip bodice on doll with opening in front; lap pressed edge over raw edge. Slip-stitch in place around arms, neck, front, and bottom with all raw edges tucked inside.

For shawl, hem long edge. Draw out threads along other two edges for fringe. Wrap and drape shawl around peddler's shoulders; slip-stitch in place at front.

For bonnet, fold in half as indicated with right sides facing, then stitch around curved and angled edge from dot to bottom edge; clip to seamline where indicated. Press one long edge of bonnet facing 1/4″ to wrong side. With right sides together, stitch raw edge of facing to open edge of bonnet. Fold pressed edge of facing over to wrong side of bonnet and slip-stitch in place, covering stitching line. Hem bottom edge. Place bonnet on peddler's head; secure with pins if necessary.

Following *Glasses Diagram*, bend length of black wire into

shape. Stitch to peddler's nose.

To make tray, use X-acto knife to cut two 1 3/8 × 2 1/4″ pieces from basswood; also cut two 1 3/8 × 1/4″ strips and two 2 1/4 × 1/4″ strips. Cut four 5 1/2″ lengths of gold pearl cotton. Measure 1/4″ away from each long edge of one tray piece; glue pearl cotton to tray following *Tray Diagram*. Glue tray pieces together, securing pearl cotton in between. With bottom edges even, glue strips to tray so edges meet at corners and pearl cotton ties are inside tray; trim away excess wood at corners if necessary so strips meet neatly. Let dry.

To make baby dolls in tray, cut three 3″-diameter circles of muslin. Add wad of fiberfill to center of each circle, then tie thread around circle and fiberfill, forming a 1/2″-diameter ball for each head. Paint heads flesh, then add rosy cheeks and red mouth as for peddler. Using rapidograph pen or felt-tipped marker, make two dots for eyes. Cut a small piece of eyelet trim and wrap around head so scalloped edge frames face; sew under chin. Following *Baby Doll Diagram*, cut small piece of fabric. Position head on fabric as shown, then wrap fabric around body following arrows. Slip-stitch at front securely, folding raw edges inside. Sew one white bugle bead and one seed bead to front of each baby doll. Glue one doll to peddler's hand; glue other two dolls to tray. Bend peddler's arm holding the doll upward as shown in photograph; secure with a stitch through the

sleeve. Arrange three square beads in a pyramid to resemble blocks; glue together. Using rapidograph pen, write A, B, and C on beads. Glue pyramid of beads to tray. Cut satin ribbon in half. Tie into two bows; glue bows to tray. Tie pearl cotton strings around peddler's neck so tray extends outward.

To make bead dolls, cut three 4″ lengths of wire. Following *Bead Doll Diagram*, for each doll insert wire through a seed bead; fold wire in half with bead at fold. Insert both ends of wire through jewelry finding, with finding facing either up for a crown or down for a cap. Insert both wire ends through beige-colored square bead, then separate wires for arms. For each arm, insert wire through one bugle and one seed bead, then bend wire back through the bugle bead. Twist wires together below neck. Draw face on square bead using rapidograph pen. For dress, cut a triangle of fabric, and clip off the tip of the triangle. Wrap around doll with clipped edge at neck; wrap matching thread around neck to secure dress. Add a contrasting yoke if desired with a small rectangle of fabric. Sew seed bead buttons to front. Attach bead dolls to a 4″ length of pearl cotton, then glue the end of the pearl cotton to peddler's free hand. Sew loop of white thread to top of peddler's head for hanging.

The Scandinavian Tree

Certain animals have always been associated with Christmas. Every manger scene has its cows and sheep peering innocently over the shoulders of Mary and Joseph. Anyone with a rural background can probably conjure up the memory of a sleek brown high-stepping horse, his breath making plumes of smoke in the cold air, pulling a sleigh to the accompaniment of harness bells. And, as we all know, a team of reindeer, guided by Rudolf's bright nose, pulls Santa's sleigh across the sky each Christmas Eve.

Goats, however, are not usually considered Christmas animals—unless one is from Scandinavia. Because despite differences in the appearance of decorated trees in Sweden, Norway, and Denmark, one decoration—a straw billy goat called a *Julbuk*—is found on all of them.

Julbuks are made in all different sizes. Some are small enough to hang on a tree, while others stand, in obstinate billy goat fashion, on the floor before it. The body is straw wrapped around a cardboard tube stuffed with newspapers; the legs and head are woven-straw sheaves attached to the body with a piece of stiff wire. A pair of braided straw horns provides the crowning touch.

The story of the *Julbuk* begins around the bonfires of ancient pagan celebrations such as *Joulu*, which took place each December to celebrate the return of the sun. (The Scandinavian word *Jul*, in fact, is derived from *Joulu* and is the source of our word *Yule*.) Originally fashioned as an effigy of one of the sacred goats of Thor, the Norse god of thunder, the *Julbuk* was carried during religious rituals by a man dressed in a goatskin and a goat mask. No one quite knows how it became a Christmas ornament (both the Catholic and Protestant churches banned it as a form of devil worship), but it reflects that peculiar mixture of pagan and Christian customs that gives a Scandinavian Christmas celebration such vitality.

Although the Scandinavian countries all celebrate Christmas in a similar manner, each has added its own accent to the decorated tree. Decorated trees came to Scandinavia from Germany in the eighteenth century and first appeared in Sweden. Because the Swedish people consider an overdecorated tree a sign of bad taste, their tree is a simple but often whimsical combination of ornaments made from a few basic materials. *Julbuks* are just one species of a small barnyard of straw dolls called *Jul-docka* that are usually found on the Swedish tree. Keeping them company are a Santa's workshop of woven straw elves with bright red caps and cotton beards, carved wooden snowflakes, stars, and hearts, and birds with pipe-cleaner bodies, cardboard wings, and splayed straw tails.

Throughout the year, Swedish families save bits of brightly colored paper, which are used to wrap pieces of homemade caramel at Christmas. Each wrapping is given a ruffled fringe, which makes the tree appear flecked with small colorful peacocks' tails. There are also paper angels, mittens, doves, reindeer, birdhouses, and garlands of Swedish flags—a yellow cross on a blue field—strung from the tip of the tree down to the lowest branches, like a ship's pennants. Tucked in among the larger branches are yarn dolls made by winding yarn around cardboard forms and then tying it to form the torso, legs, arms, and head. The Swedes also display their talent for Christmas handicrafts by making quilled wreaths, which are woven of brightly colored fabric.

Swedish children mark off the days before Christmas with an Advent Tree, a small carved Christmas tree made of wood. Along with the tree come seven brightly painted carved wooden birds: each day during the week before Christmas, another bird is placed on the tree until Christmas Eve, when the last bird is perched on the top.

Lucy Cats are among the few edible ornaments sometimes found on the Swedish tree. These small saffron-flavored buns shaped like cats' heads are made especially for Luciadagen, or Saint Lucy's Day. It falls on December 13 and in Sweden is called Little Christmas. The day is named for Saint Lucy, an early Christian martyr, who according to a Swedish legend appeared during a famine in a shimmering white robe beneath a crown of light to bring food and drink to the starving people. On Luciadagen, one daughter in each Swedish family, the "Lucia Queen," rises early. Dressed in a flowing white gown with a red sash and wearing a crown of greenery adorned with candles, she serves each member of the family coffee and Lucy Cats, as well as gingerbread cakes in the shape of goats' heads.

Christmas in Norway is heralded by the appearance of Advent calendars in the shops and stalls along the street. The Advent calendar ticks off the days before Christmas from the first Sunday in Advent to December 24. The square for each day is covered by a shuttered casement window; when parted, it reveals a small picture in transparent colored paper, much like a stained-glass window. Some calendars are religious, showing choirs of angels or biblical scenes, while others feature folklore or secular pictures.

The decorated tree is a recent addition to the Norwegian Christmas. The custom came to Norway from Sweden in the mid-1800s, although in some remote areas of the country the first decorated trees didn't appear until the early twentieth century. One of the most striking Norwegian ornaments, a straw crown, doesn't hang from the tree at all but from the ceiling. Made of woven straw, the crown is the centerpiece of a mobile made up of a myriad of intricately balanced straw diamonds, which revolve at the slightest breeze.

Like the Swedish tree, the Norwegian tree combines pagan and Christian ornaments. At the top of the tree the Norwegians traditionally place three candles to represent the Three Wise Men. Hiding in the lower branches are straw figures of men and animals, which were originally created to represent powerful spirits believed to dwell in the grain. Garlands of Norwegian flags, small glass balls, and a multitude of paper ornaments—chains, stars, and angels of gold and silver foil—provide a colorful contrast to the straw decorations.

Straw also plays an important part in two popular Norwegian Christmas customs. On Christmas Eve, Norwegian farm families lay fresh straw on the floor in the main room of the house, where they spend the night. In the morning the straw is spread on the fields to insure a good harvest. The largest sheaf of grain from the harvest—called the *Julenek,* or Jule Tree—is also hung on a high post in the yard for the birds to eat, a custom reflecting the Norwegian belief that all God's creatures must be cared for at the time of Christ's birth.

The Danes have a special feeling for Christmas, perhaps because many Christmas fairy tales came from the pen of the Danish writer Hans Christian Andersen. That fairy-tale spirit is evident in the *Jul-nisse* that the Danes make for their trees each Christmas. *Jul-nisse* are gnomes, much like leprechauns, believed to live in the lofts and cellars of farmhouses and homes. They love children and cats and generally bring good luck into a house, but unless they are treated well, they cause mischief. At Christmas the Danes leave out a bowl of porridge to cajole the *nisse* into good behavior. *Nisse* ornaments are little men dressed in gray homespun with red bonnets, long red stockings, and white clogs.

Like the Swedes and Norwegians, the Danes decorate the tree with their flag, a white cross on a red field. (As a composite, our tree is decorated with the flags of all three nations.) Favorite ornaments among children are heart-shaped baskets, made of glazed paper, which are filled with Christmas candy and crackers, gingerbread soldiers, and mobiles made of tinsel and brightly colored paper.

Christmas cookies are a major part of any Danish Christmas, although most are not hung on the tree. Rather they are eaten off blue-and-white *Julaften* plates. Now a Danish tradition, these plates date from the days when wealthy families gave their servants plates of cakes and cookies at Christmas. Decorated with Danish scenes and holiday customs, the plates were finer than any the servants had; consequently, they were treasured and brought out only at Christmas. Traditional Danish Christmas cookies include *klejner,* made of butter and sugar and fried in a saucepan of oil until pale brown, and *brunekager,* made by rolling out dough until it covers the top of the kitchen table. Circles are cut from the dough with a glass jar, and the cookies are baked with an almond half placed on top of each one.

In all three Scandinavian countries, Christmas is the longest and most festive holiday; it lasts until January 13, which is King Knut's Day, named after the Norse ruler who set aside twenty days for celebrating *Jul.* On that day, the tree is stripped of its ornaments and carried out of the house to the accompaniment of a song: "After twenty days of Knut,/We dance the Christmas tree out."

WOODEN SANTA

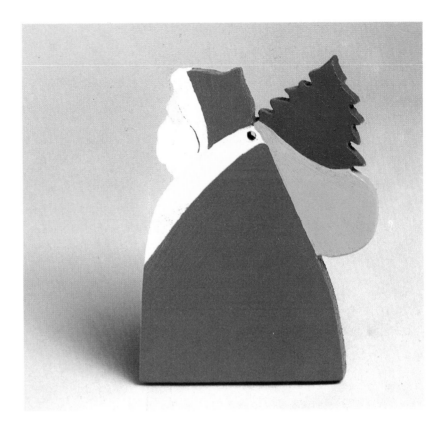

NOTE: Before beginning, read General Directions for Transferring Designs on page 14 and General Directions for Woodworking on page 15 for additional materials and directions.

Skill Level: Elementary.

Materials: 1/4″ basswood, one 4 × 22″ sheet. Acrylic paints: colors listed in *Color Key*. Clear-drying varnish. Drill with 1/16″ bit. Medium paintbrushes. Graphite paper. Silver cord for hanging.

Directions: Trace pattern for Santa; transfer outline only to basswood. Cut out using jig or coping saw. Mark exact position for hanging hole, indicated by open circle, on basswood. Using 1/16″ bit, drill hole. Sand; dust with tack cloth. Transfer design onto front and back using graphite paper. Paint both sides with acrylic paints, following *Color Key* and allowing paint to dry thoroughly before painting an adjacent color. Paint side edges, continuing lines of color from front and back. Varnish both sides of ornament. Insert silver cord through hanging hole, and tie into a loop.

COLOR KEY

R *red*

G *green*

W *white*

Y *yellow/orange*

F *flesh*

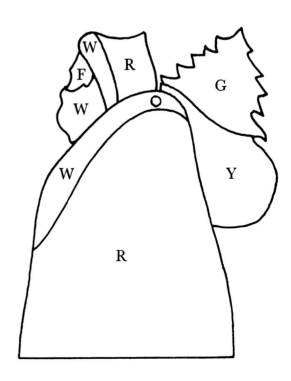

79

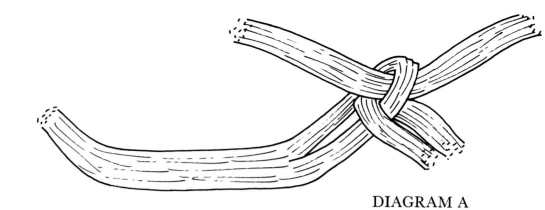

DIAGRAM A

DIAGRAM B

DIAGRAM C

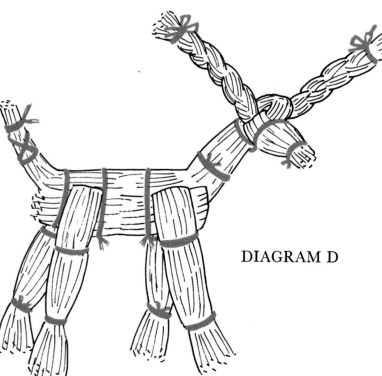

DIAGRAM D

JULBUK

Skill Level: Elementary.

Materials: Dried straw. Red yarn. Scissors. Tape measure. Transparent nylon thread for hanging.

Directions: Separate lengths of straw into neat bundles, each about 1/4″ in diameter. For upper body, cut one bundle of straw 14″ long; for snout, cut one bundle 3″ long; for horns, cut one bundle 5 1/2″ long. Fold 14″ bundle in half and bend ends upward following *Diagram A;* insert snout and horns through fold as shown. For lower body, cut one thick bundle of straw 3″ long and about 1/2″ in diameter; for legs, cut four bundles, each 6″ long. Following *Diagrams B* and C, fold body and leg bundles in half and insert legs through body. Tie legs with red yarn to secure. Following *Diagram D*, attach upper body to lower body by tying with yarn. Braid horns; secure with yarn. Tie tail, snout, and neck with yarn and twist head to one side, as shown. Thread transparent thread through straw at mid-body to make loop for hanging.

WOODEN GIRLS

NOTE: Before beginning, read General Directions for Transferring Designs on page 14 and General Directions for Woodworking on page 15 for additional materials and directions.

Skill Level: Elementary.

Materials: (for three girls) 1/4″ basswood, one 4 × 22″ sheet. Dowels: 1/8″ and 3/8″ diameter. White glue. Drill with 1/16″ bit. Acrylic paints: colors listed in *Color Key*. Clear-drying varnish. Paintbrushes, medium and fine. Black felt-tipped fine-line marking pen. Graphite paper. Red six-strand embroidery floss. Gold thread for hanging.

Directions: Trace patterns; transfer outlines only to basswood. Draw three bases on basswood, each 3/4 × 3 1/2″. Cut out all pieces using jig or coping saw. Cut two 1 7/8″ lengths of 1/8″-diameter dowel for carriage handles; cut two wheels for duck, each 1/8″ thick, from 3/8″-diameter dowel. Mark exact position for hanging hole, indicated by black dot, on duck and on each girl; using 1/16″ bit, drill hole in each. Sand; dust each piece with tack cloth. Transfer entire design onto front and back of each piece using graphite paper. Paint both sides with acrylic paint following *Color Key* and photograph; allow paint to dry thoroughly before painting an adjacent color. Paint side edges, continuing lines of color from front and back. Paint pink cheeks on faces; use black marker to draw in features on all faces, including cat; draw in a black eye on duck. Dab polka dots on dresses as shown in photograph. For shaded areas (behind candle and between legs), paint a dark color to indicate a background. Paint 1/8″-diameter dowels yellow for carriage handles; paint duck wheels red. Paint two green bases and one blue base. Varnish both sides of each piece.

When dry, glue girls and their pets or carriage to base as shown in photograph. Glue handles to carriage and girl's hand. Glue wheels to duck and base. Using embroidery floss, tie red bow around duck's neck; using gold thread, tie leash through girl's hand and duck's neck following pattern. Run 7″ length of gold thread through each hanging hole; knot ends.

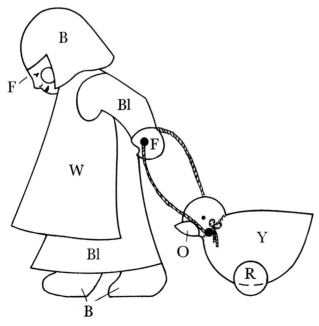

COLOR KEY

W   *white*
P   *pink*
F   *flesh*
Gn *green*
R   *red*
G   *gray*
Y   *yellow*
B   *brown*
O   *orange*
L   *light blue*
Bl *blue*

SOLDIER COOKIES

Skill Level: Elementary.

Materials: Dough. Icing. Paper for pattern. Darning needle (optional). Paintbrushes, medium and fine. Toothpicks. Ribbon or yarn for hanging.

Recipes:

DOUGH

1/2 cup softened butter or margarine
1/2 cup sugar
2 eggs
1/2 tsp. vanilla
1 1/2 cups unsifted all-purpose flour
3/4 tsp. double-acting baking powder
1/4 tsp. salt

1. Combine softened butter or margarine and sugar and beat until creamy.
2. Add eggs and vanilla, beating well.
3. Add flour, baking powder, and salt and beat until well mixed.
4. Form into ball and chill for three hours.

ICING

2 egg whites
3/8 tsp. cream of tartar
1 1/4 cups confectioner's sugar
Food coloring: red, blue, green, yellow

1. Beat egg whites with whisk or electric beater until frothy and slightly thickened.
2. Add cream of tartar and continue beating until whites hold a peak.

3. Sift confectioner's sugar into whites, about 1/2 cup at a time, beating thoroughly between additions.
4. Beat 5–8 minutes until icing is thick and smooth.
5. Set aside portion (about 1/7) that will remain white. Tint small portions of decorative icing in several small bowls by combining with food coloring until desired color is achieved (follow instructions on food coloring box to obtain desired colors). Make red, blue, light brown, yellow, flesh, and black icing.
6. Keep damp cloth over each bowl to prevent drying.

Directions:

1. Preheat oven to 350°F.
2. Trace pattern for soldier on paper.
3. Roll out ball of dough to 1/4″ thickness.

4. Place soldier pattern on dough and trace around edges with knife or darning needle; remove pattern. Punch small hanging hole near center top. Repeat until all dough is used. Place cookies on sheets.
5. Bake for 8–10 minutes or until golden brown.
6. Cool on rack.
7. Using medium paintbrush, spread surface of cooled cookies with white decorative icing that has been thinned with 2 tsp. water.
8. Use toothpick to define design in areas to be painted.
9. Paint these areas with appropriate colors of tinted icing following pattern. Draw in black eyes and red mouth using food coloring.
10. Thread hanging hole with yarn or ribbon; knot ends.
Yield: 2 dozen.

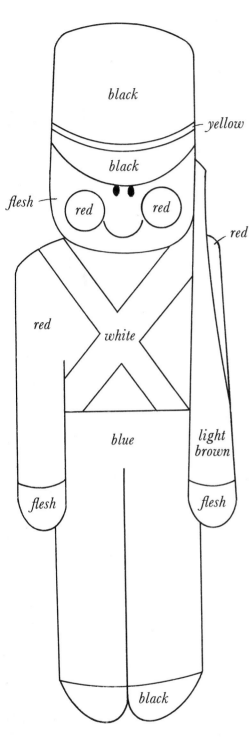

black

yellow

black

flesh

red   red

red

red

white

blue

light brown

flesh   flesh

black

YULE TREE
(*Julenek*)

Skill Level: Elementary.

Materials: Bundle of dried grasses, about 8″ long. Straight twig, 5″ long. Oven-bake modeling compound. Acrylic paints: desired colors. Fine wire. Red satin ribbon 1/4″ wide, 1/3 yard. Fine wire for hanging.

BIRD SCULPTING DIAGRAMS

Directions: Fashion two birds from modeling compound following actual-size *Sculpting Diagrams*. Bake for 15 minutes in a 325° F. oven, checking often to prevent scorching. Remove. When cool, paint as desired.

Gather bundle of dried grasses, and wire stalks together about 1 1/2″ above ends. Wire bundle to center of twig. Tie red ribbon into a bow over wiring. Glue birds to dried grasses. Wire to branch.

WOVEN HEART BASKETS

Skill Level: Elementary.

Materials: Glossy paper: one light color, one dark. Scissors. X-acto knife. White glue. Pencil. Ruler.

Directions: Trace pattern and use to cut two heart pieces, one each from light and dark paper. Using ruler and X-acto knife, slash each piece along solid lines. Fold in half, right sides out, along dash line. Position folded shapes on work surface as shown in *Diagram A*. Weave strips as shown in *Diagrams B* and *C*. When weaving is completed, straighten woven sections by pulling gently in both directions, being careful not to tear the paper.

For handle, cut strip of matching paper, 1 1/4 × 7 1/2″. Fold in half lengthwise; glue ends inside basket at inner points of heart as in *Diagram C*. Fill with candy.

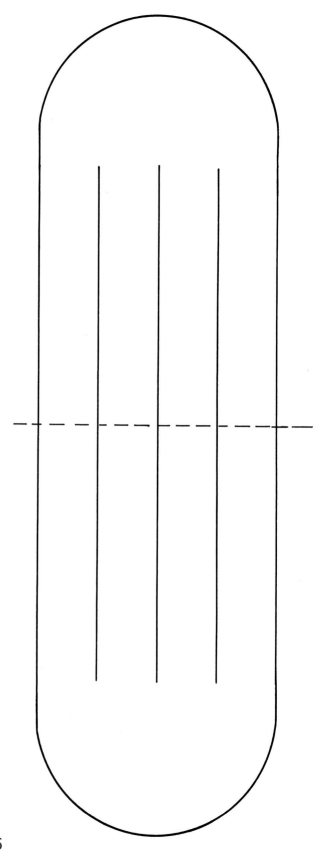

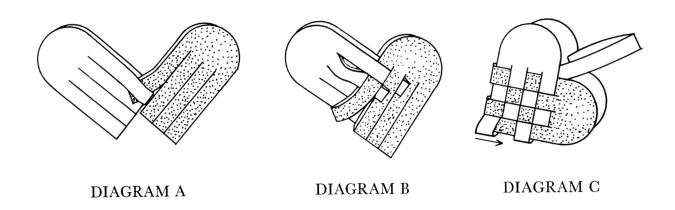

DIAGRAM A   DIAGRAM B   DIAGRAM C

CLAY SNOWFLAKES

NOTE: Before beginning, read General Directions for Ceramics on page 14 for additional materials and directions.

Skill Level: Intermediate.

Materials: Pre-wedged porcelain clay that fires to cone 06. Two 1/4″ lattice strips. Transparent overglaze. Satin ribbon for hanging.

Directions: Trace pattern onto cardboard; cut out, including inner sections. Roll slab of clay between 1/4″ lattice strips. Use pattern to cut snowflake shapes from clay; use trimming needle to remove inner sections of design entirely.

Allow ornaments to dry leather hard, then bisque-fire to cone 06. Dip in transparent overglaze; clean glaze from one hole of snowflake, then hang on rod in kiln to fire. Fire to required cone. Thread satin ribbon through cleaned hole; tie for hanging loop.

DIAGRAM A

DIAGRAM B

QUILLED WREATH

Skill Level: Elementary.

Materials: Quilling paper 1/8" wide: 3 shades of green. Corsage or hat pin. Ruler. Scissors. White craft glue that dries clear. Flat toothpick for gluing. Waxed paper. Green florist's wire. Red seed beads. Red satin ribbon 1/4" wide, 1/4 yard. Metallic gold thread.

Directions: *Technique:* Work with clean hands to prevent the paper from getting dirty. Take one strip of quilling paper and pinch one end around the corsage pin. Roll the paper tightly around the pin to produce a small round center; continue rolling the entire strip. Remove the pin and relax the tension very slightly on the roll, allowing the roll to open up (*Diagram A*); glue the loose end in place. Following *Diagram B*, pinch the roll to form the petal shape.

Wreath: On waxed paper surface, shape a 2 3/4"-diameter circle from florist's wire; twist ends together. Twist a second wire around the shaped circle, making a sturdy armature. Using different shades of quilling paper, make enough petals to fit around the interior and exterior of armature. Glue bases of petals to armature, with petals nestling closely next to each other and points of petals facing away from the armature; excess glue on waxed paper will be removed when paper is peeled away at end. Alternate colors randomly as you progress. For interior of circle, glue extra petals to those already in place, always with the points of the petals facing inward. Next, shape more petals and glue over armature and base of petals, angling and pointing petals in different directions for depth; see photograph. When dry, peel back waxed paper and glue clusters of seed beads at random to petals.

Tie satin ribbon into a bow; glue to wreath at bottom. Run 6" length of gold metallic thread around armature at top; tie ends together for hanging loop.

The Pennsylvania Dutch Tree

The story of the decorated tree in America begins in the rolling farmland of south central Pennsylvania. This is called the Pennsylvania Dutch country, although the people who began settling the area in the seventeenth century were not Dutch at all, but German. (The word *Dutch* is a mispronunciation of *Deutsch*.) Among the things the settlers brought with them on the long Atlantic crossing was the custom of having a decorated tree at Christmastime.

By the 1820s decorated trees were fairly common in the larger towns of the Pennsylvania Dutch country, such as Lancaster and Carlisle. Twenty years later, they were no longer a novelty even in small villages, and in a foreshadowing of the future, some people had already realized that Christmas could be profitable: in 1836 a group of clever women, all members of a charitable society, set up a decorated tree in the organization's headquarters in York, Pennsylvania, and charged visitors 6 1/2 cents to see it. By all accounts, the exhibit was a sellout.

In the Pennsylvania Dutch country of the 1820s, there were few stores, and little money to spend in them. At Christmas people took time out from their strenuous daily chores and exercised their imaginations to create ornaments for the family tree. From the carved wooden star or angel gracing its top to the manger scene beneath it, the Pennsylvania Dutch tree has handmade and homemade written all over it. It reflects the resourceful spirit of a people living close to the land and their determination, despite their limited means, to celebrate Christmas with a simple yet beautiful tree.

Pennsylvania Dutch women were fine bakers, and in the weeks before Christmas, a Noah's Ark of animals in the form of cookies and savory cakes issued from their kitchens to be hung on the tree. *Matzebaum* was a particular favorite. Made from almond paste, sugar, and egg whites, these rectangular cakes were decorated with cameo images of goats, cows, chickens, cats, and rabbits. Flowers and songbirds were also popular designs, and all were created by pressing handcarved wooden molds—no Pennsylvania Dutch kitchen was complete without a set—into the dough. The almond paste in these delightful confections was expensive, and with one eye on the pocketbook the thrifty Pennsylvania Dutch housewife would make some of the dough by mixing cornmeal or wheat flour with glue to produce an inexpensive, but also inedible, version of the same cookie. After baking, both the edible and inedible *matzebaum,* as well as most of the other cookies destined for the tree, were painted bright colors with dyes made from vegetables and wild berries.

Springerle cookies were as popular as *matzebaum* for ornaments. Like *matzebaum,* they were decorated with a cameo image on one side made with carved wood or tin molds but were pressed into egg dough seasoned with anise. (Today these *springerle* molds, particularly the wooden ones, are collectors' items.)

The Swiss-German settlers in this region favored *tirggel* as Christmas cookies and as ornaments. Made from honey, flour, and sugar, these wafer-thin marvels were prized for their near-translucence. They were often hung on the tree in front of a candle, which would highlight the cameo image on the front of the cookie, much as a stenciled pattern on a window is clearly outlined when a light source is placed behind it.

One cookie baked exclusively as a decoration was *tragant.* It was made with a fine-grained, hard, durable dough that lent itself to painting or icing. The name comes from tragacanth, a gum mixed into the dough that gave it a puttylike consistency perfect for molding baskets, birds, flowers, trumpets, and Christ Child dolls. *Tragants* were dried in the oven and then decorated with colored sugar icing. Hanging on the tree, they provided a feast for the eyes, but unfortunately not for the mouth.

With so many cookie ornaments, it would seem that there was hardly room for anything else on the tree, which at first was only some four feet high because it stood on a table. (Later, larger firs became popular and were placed on the floor in a large tub of earth.) But the tree held much more: its green needles literally disappeared under a cornucopia of other ornaments. The most popular of these were *schnitz,* dried apples in the shape of quarter moons, which were strung together and wrapped around the tree, as were strings of almonds, raisins, and popcorn. Branches drooped under the weight of sugarplums, which were made by boiling greengage plums in a thick syrup of cornstarch and sugar until they became translucent and preserved.

Nature, with an assist from the lively Pennsylvania Dutch imagination, also provided many ornaments. One of the most beautiful yet simple was an early version of the Christmas ball made by wrapping a walnut in tin foil and suspending it from the tree with a bit of thread. And if foil wasn't available, walnuts could be decorated, again using vegetable dyes, with brightly colored abstract designs. Hollow eggshells were also decorated in this fashion and hung on the tree, or, in a technique called decalcomania, had pictures affixed to them. One clever person, a Doctor M. L. Herr of Lancaster, even fashioned a four-horse team complete with harnesses and reins out of eggshells using the decalcomania technique. Much simpler were the homemade stuffed animals that dangled from branches here and there. For a final touch, the tree might be sprinkled with a mixture of water and flour, and then dusted with sugar to make it appear frosted.

And still there was room for presents. "Grandfather's Christmas Tree," an article by Henry Harbaugh that appeared in *The Guardian*, a Pennsylvania Dutch country newspaper, relates how "all the little presents, for all the members of the family, are also hung on the branches. There hang handkerchiefs, collars, little red shoes, speckled stockings, little books, candy baskets, dolls, little men and little horses, and little whips and wagons. . . ."

On Christmas Eve children left straw baskets with hay in them beneath the tree. The hay was for the mule of the *Christkind,* or Christ Child, who, the children were told, brought the gifts that magically appeared during the night. The gifts themselves were called *Christkindlies* and might include, for boys, miniature horses and wagons handcarved of wood, boots, and toy soldiers and, for girls, thimbles, scissors, and wax dolls.

The area beneath the tree was a Christmas world all its own. It was re-served for a manger scene, or *putz*—the name comes from the German verb *putzen,* which means to decorate. The first *putzes* were created by the Moravians who settled in the area around Bethlehem, Pennsylvania, in the 1700s. In the hands of the Pennsylvania Dutch, the *putz* became a Lilliputian landscape. Each November, moss was dug up and replanted in the cellar, and at Christmas it was used to carpet the area around the trunk of the tree. Rocks and twigs draped with moss fashioned a realistic scene around the manger, which was filled with clay figures and animals.

As time went on, people began to make *putzes* that recreated their rural world in miniature. Small farms with buildings of decorated gingerbread were enlivened with clay animals and men and women made of hickory nuts or turkey wishbones. And to give the scene a touch of homely realism, it was often glazed with sugar to suggest a winter landscape.

Taking down the tree today is often a melancholy occasion. Nothing symbolizes the end of the holiday—and the evaporation of that bustling, excited atmosphere that descends like magic each December—than a dried-out Christmas tree propped outside a house. For the Pennsylvania Dutch, however, taking down the tree was like a second helping of dessert. It was usually done on Twelfth Night, January 6, when the tree would be stripped of its edible decorations, which we can be sure were consumed with relish.

STUFFED MOUSE

NOTE: Before beginning, read General Directions for Sewing on page 15.

Skill Level: Advanced.

Materials: Muslin 36″ wide, 1/2 yard. Matching calico fabric 36″ wide, 1/8 yard. White ruffled eyelet trim 2 1/2″ wide, 7″ length. Pink gingham ribbon 1/2″ wide, 6″ length. Tape measure. Scissors. Compass. Sewing needle. White thread. Polyester fiberfill. Acrylic paints: red, pink, white, brown, gray, orange, yellow, green. Paintbrushes, medium and fine. Black rapidograph pen. Felt-tipped fine-line marking pens, red and green. Medium-weight green wire. Walnut. 1/4″ basswood, 2 1/4 × 5″ piece. White glue. Circle from white paper doily, about 1 1/2″ diameter. Two black seed beads. Plastic fishing line, about 1/4 yard.

Directions: Cut the following from muslin: two legs, one 4 × 6 1/2″ body, two 1 × 2″ arms, one 1 1/2 × 5 1/2″ tail, one 5 1/2″-diameter head, two 1 1/2″-diameter ears, one 7″-diameter mobcap, one 3 3/4 × 2″ apron, one 1 × 12″ waistband, one 1 × 5″ neck-band. From calico, cut one 3 3/4 × 15″ dress and two 2 1/4 × 2 3/4″ sleeves.

Stitch long edges of body piece together, forming a tube; machine-baste 1/4″ from each raw edge. Pull basting at one edge, gathering fabric tightly; tie off. Turn body to right side; stuff with fiberfill until firm. Pull basting around raw edge, gathering fabric tightly and enclosing fiberfill; tie off for neck.

For each leg, press seam allowance to wrong side, clipping curves as necessary; clip along dash line to large dot. To shape lower leg, roll fabric to wrong side in direction of arrow; slip-stitch pressed edge over rolled fabric. Pin haunch section of leg to each side of body slightly toward the front (area opposite seam). Stuff haunch lightly with fiberfill and slip-stitch in place.

For head, fill center of circle with fiberfill, then gather raw edges together and wrap thread around fabric, forming a 1 1/4″-diameter ball; ball should be stuffed to medium firmness. Holding the ball with the tied-off neck down, shape the face as follows: Pinch the fabric and some fiberfill, forming a pointed, triangular snout, and stitch from side to side following *Snout Diagram*. Following *Mouth Diagram,* press down on the snout and pinch and tack any folds that form below the nose. Run needle through the indentation formed, bringing point of the needle out through the eyes, and pulling thread tightly with each stitch. Next, run needle back and forth between the eyes, drawing that section of the head together as shown in *Face Diagram.* When satisfied with head, sew one black seed bead in each eye indentation. Stitch head firmly to body, hiding tied-off edges.

Make ears as follows: Fold each circle in half; hand-baste close to raw edges, then pull basting, gathering ears tightly at base. Ear will naturally indent from the gathering; adjust indentation evenly for the inside of the ear.

For arms, fold each in half, matching long edges. Stitch across long edge and one short edge; turn to right side and stuff with fiberfill. Push raw edges inside and slip-stitch closed. Set aside. For tail, press one long edge 1/4″ to wrong side; roll raw edge toward pressed edge; slip-stitch pressed edge over rolled section of tail; stitch tail in place on body.

Paint mouse with acrylic paints highly diluted with water; test colors on scrap fabric before actually painting the soft sculpture. Paint red mouth with white teeth; paint white highlight on each eye. Paint nose, snout, and interior of ears pink. Paint remainder of head, body, arms, ears, and tail light gray with brown flecks. Using rapidograph pen, draw in fine lines for hair on face and ears; extend edges of eyes for an almond shape; see *Face Diagram.* Bend green wire into eyeglass shape, following actual-size pattern. Stitch glasses to face below eyes. For whiskers, cut three 4″ lengths of fishing line; run each length evenly through bulbous portion of snout. Knot whiskers close to fabric on each side; trim.

For slip, stitch ends of eyelet lace trim together; pull on body with seam in back; slip-stitch in place, pleating

SNOUT DIAGRAM

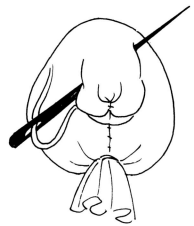

MOUTH DIAGRAM

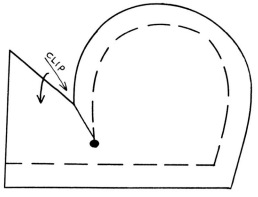

LEG

EYEGLASSES

FACE DIAGRAM

95

fabric if necessary so fit is secure. For dress, stitch short ends of calico fabric together; press seam open. Make 1/4" hem at each long edge; hand-baste 1/8" from one hemmed edge. Slip dress on mouse with seam at back and basted edge at neck. Pull basting, gathering dress tightly around neck; tie off basting. For sleeves, stitch long edges of each, making two tubes; turn to right side. Fold raw edges at each end 1/4" to wrong side; hand-baste close to all folded edges. Slip one arm inside each sleeve; pull basting tightly and stitch sleeve to arm, completely covering one end (upper arm). Pull basting at opposite end tightly around wrist, leaving 1/4" exposed for hand; slip-stitch in place. Draw fingers with rapidograph pen. Stitch sleeves and upper arms to dress and body in shoulder area.

For apron, hem one long edge and two short edges of muslin piece; baste across remaining long edge. Gather upper edge of apron to 2" width; tie off basting. Press long edges of waistband and neckband 1/4" to wrong side, then press in half with raw edges inward. Find center of waistband; sandwich apron between pressed edges of waistband at center; topstitch in place. Continue topstitching across remainder of waistband, forming ties. Topstitch folded edges of neckband in same manner. Tie apron on mouse just below arms; arrange neckband around back of mouse's neck so that ends are tucked inside waistband; slip-stitch in

place. Using red and green felt-tipped markers, draw a tiny floral border along edges of waistband and neckband; see photograph.

For mobcap, press raw edges of circle 3/4" to wrong side, clipping fabric if necessary. Machine-baste 1/2" from pressed edge, securing raw edge of fabric. Pull basting, gathering hat to fit on mouse's head; tie off basting and tack mobcap to head where necessary. Tack ears to mobcap in correct position, hiding raw edges. Tie gingham ribbon into a bow; tack to mobcap between ears.

Using oven-bake modeling compound, shape eight 1/4"-diameter balls for oranges; form about ten irregular shapes for kernels of popcorn. Bake for 15 minutes in a 325° F. oven; allow to cool, then paint balls orange and kernels white with yellow highlights. Pierce four oranges and three kernels of popcorn with needle; thread alternately on 7" length of green wire. Open walnut, leaving at least one half of shell intact; remove nut. Glue one orange to mouse's right hand; glue remaining oranges and kernels inside walnut.

Paint basswood green. Glue paper doily near one short end; glue walnut in center of doily. Glue mouse, tilted slightly toward the walnut, to opposite end of basswood. Pierce mouse's left hand with one end of the wire; bend wire over about 2" so it is secure on hand. Glue orange or kernel at opposite end of wire to basswood. Nestle in branches.

GINGERBREAD CAT

Skill Level: Elementary.

Materials: Gingerbread dough. Paper for pattern. Darning needle (or knife). Red yarn. Wire for hanging.

Recipe:

GINGERBREAD DOUGH
6 cups sifted all-purpose flour
4 tsp. ground ginger
1 1/2 tsp. ground cinnamon
1 tsp. ground cloves
1/4 tsp. each: ground nutmeg, cardamom, salt
2 sticks butter or margarine
1 cup firmly packed light brown sugar
1/2 cup dark corn syrup
1/2 cup light molasses

1. Sift flour and spices together in bowl.
2. Combine butter, brown sugar, corn syrup, and molasses in saucepan and place over low heat until butter is melted and all ingredients are blended. Remove from heat.
3. Combine 2 cups flour mixture and the butter mixture in mixing bowl and blend well.
4. Continue adding remaining flour mixture, blending until dough is firm but pliable.
5. Flour hands and knead dough until smooth and slightly sticky. If dough is too moist, add flour by the tablespoon.
6. Refrigerate for one hour.

Directions:
1. Preheat oven to 325° F.

2. Trace pattern for cat on paper.

3. Roll out dough between sheets of waxed paper to 3/8" thickness.

4. Place cat pattern on dough and trace around edges with knife or darning needle; transfer inner lines of design to dough by pricking through the paper pattern with needle or toothpick. Remove pattern; connect dotted lines for smooth curves; remove section between front legs; punch small hanging hole near center top. Repeat until all dough is used. Place finished cookies on sheets.

5. Bake for 35 minutes or until cookies are firm and brown.

6. Cool completely.

7. Tie red yarn around neck for collar. Thread wire through hanging hole and twist ends together.

Yield: 2 dozen.

97

MATZEBAUM
(Marzipan)
POTATOES

Skill Level: Elementary.

Materials: *For Marzipan:*
1 lb. pure almond paste; 1 1/2
cups sifted confectioner's sugar;
3 tbsp. light corn syrup; 3/4 tsp.
vanilla.
Also: Cinnamon. Toothpick.
Needle. Gold thread for hanging.

Directions: Mix marzipan ingredients together and knead
until smooth. Break off pieces
of marzipan and roll into 1″-
diameter shapes resembling
potatoes; do not make balls
perfectly round. When satisfied
with shape, roll in cinnamon.
Insert toothpick through one
end of each potato for hanging
hole. Allow potatoes to harden,
then thread needle with 7″
length of gold thread. Run
needle and thread through
hanging hole; knot ends.
Yield: 4 dozen.

CLAY WINTER
PEAR

*NOTE: Before beginning, read
General Directions for Ceramics on
page 14 for additional materials
and directions.*

Skill Level: Intermediate.

Materials: Pre-wedged porcelain clay that fires to cone 06.

Watercolor paints: pink, green.
Fine wire for hanging loop.
Glue. Shellac (optional). Satin
ribbon 1/8″ wide, 6″ length.

Directions: Shape winter
pear following actual-size
Sculpting Diagram: include leaf
at top if desired. Bend and twist
wire into loop as shown in
diagram; insert into top of
pear, then remove. Allow pear
to become bone dry, then fire
to cone 06. Apply watercolor
paints to pear, following photograph. Glue twisted-wire loop
into previously made hole.
Shellac pear if desired. Thread
ribbon through wire loop; tie
ends together.

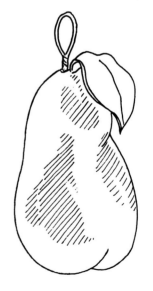

CLAY WINTER PEAR
SCULPTING DIAGRAM

98

COOKIES WITH PAPER CUTOUTS

Skill Level: Elementary.

Materials: Dough. Icing. Ruler. Paper for pattern. Knife. Darning needle (optional). Prints of angels or other motifs. Curved cuticle scissors. Paintbrush for icing. Gold ribbon.

Recipes: Refer to Dough Recipe for Gingerbread Cat on page 96. Refer to Icing Recipe for Soldier Cookies on page 84; halve the recipe and add 2 tablespoons of water. Make icing while gingerbread bakes; cover with damp towel to prevent drying. (Icing will be used to attach the cutouts to each baked cookie.)

Directions:
1. Preheat oven to 325° F.
2. On paper, draw a rectangle 3 1/4 × 4″; round the corners. Cut out pattern.
3. Roll out dough between sheets of waxed paper to 1/2″ thickness.
4. Place pattern on dough and trace around edges with knife or darning needle; remove pattern. Punch small hanging hole near center top of one short edge. Repeat until all dough is used. Place cookies on sheets.
5. Bake for 35 minutes or until cookies are firm and brown.
6. Cool completely.
7. While cookies are baking and cooling, carefully cut out prints using curved cuticle scissors. When cookies are cool, cover the back of the print with a thin

SUGAR RING COOKIES

Skill Level: Elementary.

Materials: Dough. Compass. Paper for pattern. Darning needle (optional). Red or green yarn or ribbons for hanging.

Recipe: Refer to Dough Recipe for Soldier Cookies on page 84.

Directions:
1. Preheat oven to 350° F.
2. On paper draw two concentric circles 3/4″ and 2 1/4″ in diameter. Cut around outer circle, then inner, leaving ring pattern.
3. Roll out ball of dough to 1/8″ thickness.
4. Place ring pattern on dough and trace around edges with knife or darning needle; remove pattern. Repeat until all dough is used. Place cookies on sheets; leave plain or coat with colored sprinkles, tapping sprinkles lightly into the dough with the tip of your finger.
5. Bake for 8–10 minutes or until golden brown.
6. Cool on rack.
7. For each cookie, cut 7″ length of yarn or ribbon; thread through center of ring and knot ends.
Yield: 3 dozen.

layer of icing. Press the iced side of the print on the center of the cookie.

8. Thread hanging hole with gold ribbon; knot ends.

Yield: 8–10 cookies.

SPRINGERLE COOKIES

NOTE: Before beginning, read General Directions for Ceramics on page 14 for additional materials and directions.

Skill Level: Advanced.

Materials: Tracing paper. Two 1/2″ lattice strips. Pre-wedged porcelain clay that fires to cone 06. Loop. *For Cookies:* Dough. Icing. Fine and medium paintbrushes. Toothpick. Gold metallic paint (optional). Gold thread for hanging.

Directions: *For Mold:* Trace springerle outline onto heavy cardboard and cut out. Trace entire design on tracing paper and cut out. Roll slab of clay between 1/2″ lattice strips. Use cardboard pattern to cut shape from clay. Position traced design over shape and transfer all lines to clay by pricking holes through paper and into the clay with a trimming needle. Using loop and trimming needle, gently scrape away clay from space inside the red line (see pattern) to reveal the soldier and horse. Sculpt deeply for areas that are to stand out sharply, such as the horse and the soldier's leg. Work slowly and carefully, wetting the needle or loop if necessary to scribe clean shapes; refer often to pattern. Use trimming needle to incise lines for grass.

When satisfied with mold, allow to become bone dry before firing. Fire to cone 06.

Recipes:

DOUGH
4 cups sifted all-purpose flour
1 tsp. baking powder

1/2 tsp. salt
4 eggs
2 cups granulated sugar
2 tsp. grated orange rind

1. Sift together flour, baking powder, and salt.
2. Beat eggs, sugar, and orange rind in bowl at medium speed with electric mixer. Add flour mixture, 1/2 cup at a time. Chill in refrigerator overnight.
3. Roll dough to 5/8″ thickness on a flour-covered board.
4. Flour ceramic mold and gently press into dough. Trim around edge of mold with a knife. Remove mold; make a hole in cookie at top edge for hanging. Repeat until all dough is used.

5. Sprinkle flour on greased cookie sheet; place cookies on sheet and let stand at room temperature overnight.
6. Bake in a 325° F. oven for 15 minutes or until done.

ICING
Refer to Icing Recipe for Soldier Cookies on page 84. Reserve 1/3 portion for white; tint remaining icing the following colors: green, red, blue, yellow, flesh, brown, dark blue, black, and pale blue. (See package directions to mix colors.) Keep damp cloth over each bowl to prevent drying.

Decorating:
1. Using medium paintbrush, spread surface and sides of cooled cookies with white decorative icing that has been thinned with 2 tsp. water.
2. Use toothpick to define design in areas to be painted.
3. Paint these areas with appropriate colors of tinted icing following photograph. *Note:* If cookie will not be eaten, you may highlight hat, epaulets, blanket, and harness with gold metallic paint.
4. Thread hanging hole with gold metallic thread; knot ends. *Yield: 1 dozen.*

The Southern Tree

Christmas *in* the antebellum South was the height of the social season, a time of lavish hospitality, brightly lit plantation mansions, and an endless round of entertainment. "Nothing is now to be heard of in conversation," wrote Philip Vickers Furthian, a tutor at a large Virginia plantation, in his diary, "but the Balls, the Fox-hunts, the fine entertainments, and the good fellowship, which are to be exhibited at the approaching Christmas."

At Christmas, southern homes were filled with the fragrance of evergreens. Garlands of ivy, boxwood, laurel, or yew lined doorways and hung in swags over fireplace mantels. Young men were sent out to the woods to gather mistletoe, which, because it grew in the tops of tall trees, often had to be dislodged with a well-aimed rifle shot. Mistletoe was combined with other evergreens to form one of the most popular southern Christmas decorations, the kissing ball, a leafy sphere that hung from the ceiling. When a man kissed a woman under the kissing ball, he plucked a white berry from the mistletoe; when the berries were gone, so was the mistletoe's magic.

Long dinner tables were graced with fruit pyramids made by impaling lemons on sharp sticks, which were then stuck into three heads of cabbage placed one on top of another. Evergreens filled in the spaces between the lemons, and the pyramid was crowned with the top of a pineapple. (The lemons on the pyramid kept throughout the holidays because they had been dipped in wax.) Doorways were often adorned with a fan of apples topped with a pineapple, a decoration that symbolized traditional southern hospitality.

The decorated tree became a part of the southern Christmas in the 1840s. One of the first decorated trees in the South was set up in 1842 in the Williamsburg, Virginia, home of Judge Nathaniel Beverly Tucker by a young German named

Charles Minnegerode, a teacher at the College of William and Mary. People came from miles around to see it, and Judge Tucker liked it so much that he continued to put up a tree every year until his death.

Most southern Christmas trees resembled the one Minnegerode and Judge Tucker improvised. Strings of cranberries and popcorn wound their way around the boughs, and paper ornaments in the shape of globes, birds, and geometric patterns added splashes of color. Since glass ornaments were not available in the antebellum South, gilded pinecones were often used instead. The women of the house displayed their prowess at sewing by needle-pointing or crocheting brightly colored ornaments in abstract patterns and making small bags of white tarletan cut in heart shapes and edged with fine worsted. Tiny wreaths garnished with bayberries and chinaberries hung on the tree, and paper poinsettia flowers added dashes of festive crimson.

The poinsettia, in fact, is a uniquely southern contribution to the American Christmas. The plant is named for Joel Roberts Poinsett, the first American ambassador to Mexico. Poinsett brought the plant with him in the 1820s when he returned to his native Charleston, South Carolina, where its flamboyant Christmas blooms quickly made it a favorite.

Although Alabama, Louisiana, and Arkansas were the first three states to declare Christmas a legal holiday, the decorated tree as a Christmas custom caught on slowly there. It was most popular along the Atlantic seaboard. In 1850 the ladies of Charleston erected a Christmas tree in front of the hotel where Jenny Lind, who was there on a concert tour, was staying. At almost the same time, though, in 1851, a niece of Jefferson Davis's, Mahalia Eggleston Roach, who lived on a Mississippi plantation, wrote in her diary of the novelty of the decorated tree. "The children had such a number of gifts that I made a Christmas tree for them," she noted. "Mother, aunt, and Liz came down to see it; all said it was something new to them. I never saw one, but learned from some of the German stories I had been reading." As time passed, however, the tree became more popular, and today at Christmas, Colonial Williamsburg celebrates the holiday by lighting a community tree located just a stone's throw from Judge Tucker's old house.

PINEAPPLE ORNAMENTS

Skill Level: Elementary.

Materials: Colored construction paper. Metal pineapple form from stained-glass kit. Gold metallic spray paint. Scissors. Gold metallic thread.

Directions: Place pineapple form in center of a sheet of white construction paper. Spray with gold metallic paint. When dry, remove form; cut out pineapple 1/8″ away from edge of design. Cut 7″ length of gold metallic thread. Punch hole through top of pineapple; run gold thread through hole and knot ends.

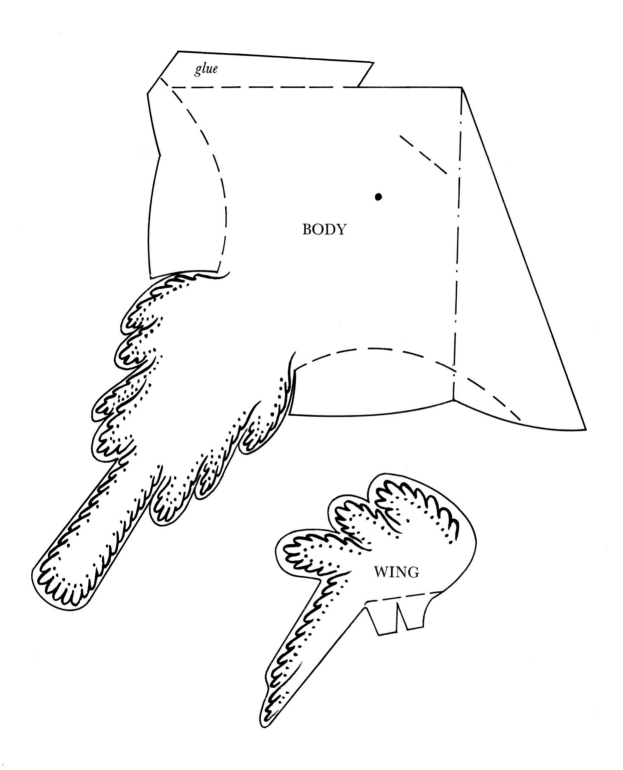

glue

BODY

WING

COLORED PAPER BIRDS

Skill Level: Elementary.

Materials: Construction paper, desired color. Scissors. White paint. Fine paintbrush. White glue. Wire for hanging.

Directions: Trace patterns and use to cut one body and two wings from construction paper. Using white paint and fine paintbrush, paint feather designs all around edges of tail and wings, following pattern. Cut 7″ length of wire; fold in half. Insert cut ends through top of bird's body at marked dot; spread wire ends open on wrong side of paper to secure. Shape folded end of wire into a hook.

To form rounded body, bend paper to wrong side along curved lines. Next, fold straight flap to wrong side and glue to opposite side of body so folded edge meets dot/dash line. Bend beak down along dash line. For wings, bend flaps to wrong side and glue to body as shown in photograph.

Kissing Ball

KISSING BALL

Skill Level: Elementary.

Materials: Medium-weight wire. Plastic foam ball, 2 1/2" diameter. Silk mistletoe. Silk flowers and leaves. Dried grasses.

Directions: Cut 7" length of wire; fold in half and twist securely. Insert cut ends firmly into plastic foam ball; bend opposite end into a hook. Considering wire hook as the "north pole," mark exact position of the "south pole," and insert mistletoe there so it hangs below ball. Wire separate small bunches of grasses and silk flowers and leaves. Insert wired ends into ball, spacing flowers evenly among the grasses; add bunches until ball is entirely covered.

DELLA ROBBIA WREATH

Skill Level: Elementary.

Materials: Dried grasses, natural color and/or desired dyed color, 5–7" lengths. Plastic lemons and/or other fruit, no larger than 1" diameter. Silk flowers and leaves. Satin ribbon: 1/8" wide, 6" length; 1/2" wide, 2/3 yard. Lightweight wire.

Directions: Arrange bunches of grasses into a 5 1/2"-diameter circle, interspersing dyed colored grasses with natural

grasses if desired; wire grasses where necessary to hold all pieces in place and to maintain circular shape. Add silk flowers and leaves all around wreath; wire in place securely, making sure wires are hidden. Wire lemons and/or other fruit around wreath. Tie 1/8" ribbon into a small bow; wire to wreath near section that will be top. Cut 12" length of 1/2" ribbon; tie into a bow and wire to wreath near bottom. Fold remaining ribbon in half; tie or sew ends together to form a hanging loop. Wire loop to top of wreath.

The German Tree in America

Christmas, *someone* once wrote, has been Germany's greatest export. German Christmas customs have over the years taken root in England and Scandinavia and, had it not been for German immigrants, the decorated tree might never have come to America. The Puritans who settled in Massachusetts in the 1600s certainly weren't having any of the custom. In 1659 they passed a decree stating that anyone caught observing Christmas in any way would be fined five shillings. Only in the Pennsylvania Dutch country had the decorated tree become popular before the 1820s.

The decorated tree didn't appear in the Boston area until the 1830s; predictably, one of the first ones was put up in 1832 in the Milton, Massachusetts, home of a German exile named Charles Follen, who taught his native language at Harvard University. One of Follen's guests that Christmas was the English novelist and economist Harriet Martineau, who was so taken with the tree that she described it in a penny pamphlet. "The tree was the top of a young fir," she wrote, "which was ornamented with moss. Smart dolls and other whimsies glittered in the evergreen, and there was not a twig which had not something sparkling upon it."

The same story was repeated in countless American cities. Homesick Germans introduced the Christmas tree to Philadelphia, Richmond, and Williamsburg, and they took the custom with them when they pushed westward. In 1851 the Reverend Henry Schwann, a minister who had been in America less than a year, put up the first decorated tree in an American church in Cleveland and almost lost his job when the congregation denounced it as a pagan custom. When a German pioneer named Gustav Koerner found himself at Christmas, 1833, in St. Clair County, Illinois, an area devoid of fir trees, he improvised a Christmas tree by decorating a sassafras tree with candles, apples, sweets, ribbons, bright scraps of paper, nuts, and polished haws, the fruit of the hawthorn tree.

Not only did the Germans introduce the tree to this country, they decorated it as well. From the 1860s until after World War II, most of the ornaments bought in America were made in Germany. In fact, an ornament still popular today, the glass Christmas ball, was invented in Lauscha, a small town nestled in the thickly forested mountains of Thuringia in southern Germany.

The invention of glass Christmas balls came about almost accidentally. In the 1820s Lauscha glassblowers often blew thick-walled glass balls, called *kügeln*, for fun. At Christmas, *kügeln* were sometimes fastened to wooden crowns and hung from the ceiling or placed on the tree. In the 1870s, though, a glassmaker named Louis Greiner-Schlottfeger discovered how to blow paper-thin *kügeln*, reputedly by blowing glass directly into a wooden cookie mold. Greiner-Schlottfeger had previously developed a formula for a silvering solution. He then combined his inventions by coating the inside of the delicate *kügeln* with the silvering solution to give it a mirrorlike shine, thereby creating one of the most popular ornaments ever. In 1890, F. W. Woolworth alone purchased 200,000 glass ornaments from Lauscha's glassblowers. By then, the small village was a one-product town.

Lauscha's glassblowers produced ornaments in an astonishing variety of shapes. Some estimate that more than 5,000 different kinds of ornaments were produced between 1870 and 1930. There were cherubs with pudgy cheeks and wavy golden hair; a small aviary of iridescent songbirds with spun-glass tails and, in one instance, three baby birds huddled in a nest no bigger than a quarter; a chubby lute with a little moon face; snowmen and Santas; gilded acorns and pears; and enough tiny glass houses and churches to create storybook German villages like Lauscha on trees all over America. New designs spilled out of the glassblowers' home workshops each year and were eagerly snapped up by American toy and ornament importers.

The German tree in America was as diverse as America itself. On the prairie, where families improvised ornaments with whatever came to hand, cornhusk dolls were popular as decorations and as presents. The dolls' faces were usually made of prunes or walnuts, and they were often dressed in bright scraps of old quilting material. Jacob's ladders made of stiff colored paper and angels cut from silver foil hung on the tree; homemade candy ornaments (*zuckersachen*) and popcorn balls held together with thick caramel were always favorites because they could be eaten when the tree was taken down.

In the cities, however, edible ornaments were slowly giving way to a variety of inexpensive store-bought decorations that were as simple as they were charming. Dresden ornaments were very popular. Made of silver- and gold-embossed cardboard, these were marvels of detail even though they were rarely larger than six inches. One gold carriage, for instance, featured horses, harnesses, a coachman with his feet stuck inside a sack to keep them warm, and, sitting in the carriage, a lady less than one inch high with a chenille collar around her neck. The animal world provided the inspiration for many Dresden ornaments: shoppers could buy a trophy room of elephant, antelope, deer, and other animal heads; all sorts of fish; golden swans; silver stags and horses; and a lumbering elephant with a red-curtained howdah on its back.

Santa Claus also made his debut on the German tree in America not long after the first department-store Santa created a sensation in Philadelphia in 1840. Santa Claus decorations were made of celluloid and became popular largely because of Clement Moore's poem "The Night Before Christmas." Santa shared the tree with wax figures of angels, which hung, hands folded in prayer, from a piece of thread or wire. They had spun-glass wings and were clothed in a garland of ribbon or tinsel. Wax figures of the infant Jesus were also popular—one was so small that it had half a nutshell for a cradle—as were figures of animals and of children standing on swings.

Since candles had always been part of German Christmas trees, the custom carried over to America. (One American magazine recommended placing four hundred of them on a twelve-foot-high tree!) Their soft glow was reflected in the tin ornaments that were among the first commercially produced Christmas decorations. The heat of the candle flame could make one of these light, geometric shapes—stars, circles with filigree borders, crosses, and spiraling icicles—revolve slowly, and those embellished with colored jewels of glass flashed beams of red or blue light as they turned. In the 1870s eight-sided lanterns with isinglass windows replaced candles on some trees. Each lantern contained a small candle like those used on birthday cakes; because they prevented the wax from dripping onto the tree, these lanterns were safer than candles.

The most beautiful ornament on the German tree in America was the Nuremberg angel at the top. Legend has it that the first Nuremberg angel was made by a German dollmaker in memory of his daughter killed during the Thirty Years War, which raged across central Europe from 1618 to 1648. The first Nuremberg angels to appear on American Christmas trees stood tall and straight with stern faces and outstretched arms; sometimes they held a wreath in each hand. Later ones were outfitted in sumptuous pleated-foil gowns and had china heads painted with pert facial expressions.

Despite such handsome and intriguing ornaments, there were some hard-hearted people who didn't like the German tree, or probably any tree for that matter. As late as 1878, a New York City newspaper reporter called the Christmas tree "an aboriginal oddity," while another, perhaps thinking the tree distracted people from the religious significance of Christmas, said it wasn't worthy of the day. Time has proven them wrong. As a writer with a different outlook predicted in 1850, the decorated tree became "one of the household gods of New England and a large portion of the states."

NUREMBERG ANGEL TOP

NOTE: Before beginning, read General Directions for Ceramics on page 14 for additional materials and directions.

Skill Level: Advanced.

Materials: *For Ceramic Head:* Pre-wedged porcelain clay that fires to cone 06. Acrylic paints: pink, red, blue, brown. Shellac. Loop. Fiberfill. *For Body:* Gold foil wrapping paper. Brown fake fur. White glue. Fancy decorative trim with gold threads and pearls 1 1/4″ wide, 2/3 yard. Decorative gold mesh trim 1 5/8″ wide, 6″ length. One baroque pearl. Scissors. 1/2″ dowel, 11″ long. Florist's wire. Thread. Needle.

Directions: *Ceramic Head:* Following actual-size *Sculpting Diagrams,* fashion a head from porcelain clay. Work slowly and carefully, wetting the needle if necessary to scribe clean shapes and smooth curves. Shape the head, making fat cheeks and rounded chin and forehead. Use loop to carve indentations for eyes. Shape tiny nose and nostrils as shown. Shape neck. Allow to dry leather hard, then carefully place layer of fiberfill over the face. Turn head over and place fiberfill and face in the palm of your hand. Using trimming needle and loop, remove excess clay from back of head, leaving a rounded cavity about 1/4" deep; work very slowly, being careful not to cut through to the sculpted side and not to press or flatten the sculpted area.

Allow head to become bone dry, then bisque-fire to cone o6. Using acrylics and paintbrush, paint cheeks and chin pink; paint in red lips, blue eyes, and brown eyebrows; outline eyes with brown. Let dry, then coat with shellac. Glue 1" of dowel behind head, with 10" of dowel extending below neck; wrap wire around neck and dowel to secure. Cut piece of fake fur to cover top, sides, and back of head, including top of dowel; shape fur to form bangs and to hang evenly on each side of face. Glue fur in place.

Body: Cut gold paper into a rectangle 10 × 30". Pleat paper across entire 30" width, making each pleat about 3/8" wide; tape ends together, forming a tube. Insert dowel inside tube; pleat paper tightly around angel's neck and wrap with wire to hold. Drape gold mesh trim over top of head so it hangs evenly on each side; whipstitch back edges together, forming a bonnet. Glue bonnet to head; glue pearl to center top of bonnet. Wrap gold and pearl trim around neck and down front of angel as shown in photograph; whipstitch where necessary to hold.

For wings, cut 5 × 15" rectangle of gold foil; pleat as for body, making pleats 1/4" wide. Using scissors, shape pleated foil to resemble wings. Glue center of wings to back of body, securing with small pieces of wire if necessary.

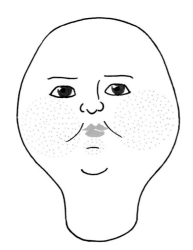

SCULPTING DIAGRAMS

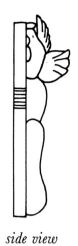

HEN

side view

BIRDCAGE

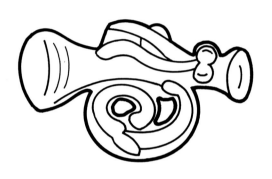

HORN

BASKET

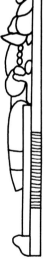

BICYCLE RIDER

side view

large wheel

PAINTED ZUCKERSACHEN

Skill Level: Intermediate.

Materials: *For All:* Salt dough (1 cup flour; 1 cup salt; water). Tracing paper. Bowl for mixing. Rolling pin. Hat pins. Knife. Acrylic paints: blue, red, green, white, yellow, orange, purple, black. Gold metallic paint. Gold thread. Wrapping paper. White glue. Polyurethane spray. *For Bicycle Rider:* Gold wrapping paper. Gold paper medallion, 1/4" diameter. Scissors. Gold sequin. Seed beads, black and white.

Directions: *For All:* Trace patterns onto tracing paper. Mix salt dough ingredients with 1 tablespoon of water; knead and add water until mixture reaches the consistency of pie dough. Roll out to 1/4" thickness using rolling pin. Place desired pattern over rolled dough and pierce main outlines (indicated by heavy lines) through pattern using hat pin. Remove pattern and cut along pin pricks with knife; wet blade often to prevent crumbling or tearing. Add dimensional de-tails, following drawings, photographs, and individual directions. Bake at 225° F. for one hour. Paint, following photographs and individual directions. When dry, make 3" hanging loop from gold thread; glue end of loop to upper back side of ornament. Using original pattern, cut backing from wrapping paper; glue to back of ornament, securing hanging loop. Coat several times with polyurethane spray.

Hen: Following side view, add dough to main shape, building up smooth, rounded lower shapes. Add dough for hen, rounding body and making

wing and tail jut out slightly as shown; incise design lines on hen with a hat pin. Bake. Paint lower shapes blue with red highlights; paint hen white with yellow beak and wing tips; paint comb and wattles red.
Basket: Carefully cut out central hole. Roll three thin, round strips of dough between the palms of your hands and press in a curved shape onto handle. Add dough to main shape below center line, building up front of basket to a 1/2" width at the center line and decreasing to 1/4" at the base; incise lines with a hat pin. Roll worms of dough between the palms of your hands, and shape into curling, twisting masses of foliage; twist some pieces tightly for flowers. Press foliage into recessed area above center of basket. Bake. Paint basket pink with green stripe on handle; paint foliage green, interspersing blue, yellow, purple, and pink flowers with green leaves.
Bicycle Rider: Carefully cut out central hole. Use pattern to cut large wheel out of gold paper; press over cut-out hole on ornament. Follow side view and photograph to sculpt bottom ledge and rider over the paper wheel. Use pin to help shape the pieces and remove excess dough; use wet fingers to round out the shapes and make them look natural. Bake. Paint lower ledge green and background white. Paint bicycle rider's coat blue; paint pants yellow with a blue stripe; paint collar and cuffs white. Paint hat pale blue, hair light

brown, and face, hands, and ankle flesh (for flesh, mix white with a few drops of red and yellow). Paint in red lips and black shoes and eye. Paint bicycle, small wheel, and pompon metallic gold; paint yellow spokes in center of small wheel. Cut 1/4"-wide strip of gold paper and glue to recessed portion at base of ledge; glue down edges of paper wheel if necessary. Glue three white seed beads to coat for buttons. Glue gold sequin to center of small wheel; glue black seed bead in center of gold sequin. Glue gold medallion to center of large wheel, trimming edge to fit neatly next to shoe.
Birdcage: Carefully cut out central hole. Roll three thin, round strips of dough between the palms of your hands and press in a curved shape onto handle; roll three more strips in same manner and press straight across cage as shown. Roll three balls of dough; press to lower portion of cage as shown. Bake. Paint horizontal strips and bars of cage yellow; paint decorative balls and bird's body orange; paint beak and tail blue; paint handle and bird's wings red, adding highlights to orange balls.
Horn: Carefully remove holes in handle. Add dough to main shape, building up a smooth, rounded handle, horn, and ribbon. Add extra dough at mouthpiece and open end of horn; carve out a recess at each end to give the piece dimension. Bake. Paint entire horn red, then paint raised portions of horn metallic gold; paint ribbon blue.

TWIN BABIES IN CARRIAGE

NOTE: Before beginning, read General Directions for Ceramics on page 14 for additional materials and directions.

Skill Level: Advanced.

Materials: *For Ceramic Heads:* Pre-wedged porcelain clay that fires to cone 06. Ceramichrome One-Stroke Translucent Underglaze, rose pink. Ceramichrome OK Dinnerware Glaze, clear gloss. Brown watercolor paint. Shellac. Loop. Stilts. *For Blanket, Pillow, and Carriage:* Pink/white fabric scrap with miniature print. 4" scrap ruffled lace trim, 3/4" wide. Compass. Scissors. White thread. Sewing needle. Pink satin ribbon 1/8" wide, 5" length. Fiberfill. White glue. Tiny straw basket with handle, about 2 1/4" diameter × 1" high. (Or a basket without handle, and bristol board.) Dowels: 1/8" and 7/8" diameter. Coping saw. Medium and fine sandpaper. Acrylic paints: white, rose, red. Paintbrush. Lightweight wire. Cord for hanging.

Directions: *Ceramic Heads:* Following actual-size *Sculpting Diagrams,* fashion two heads from porcelain clay. Work slowly and carefully, wetting the needle if necessary to scribe clean shapes and smooth curves. Shape face first, making fat cheeks and rounded chin and forehead. Use loop to carve indentations for eyes. Shape

SCULPTING DIAGRAMS

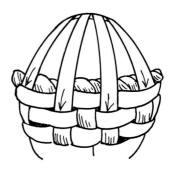

CARRIAGE HANDLE
ASSEMBLY DIAGRAM

tiny nose and nostrils. Incise wavy hair with trimming needle. Shape bonnet next, using loop and trimming needle to make wavy frills around face. Shape neck following diagram. Using pink underglaze, paint pink lips and bonnets; add touch of pink to cheeks.

When satisfied with both heads, allow pieces to become bone dry, then bisque-fire to cone 06, propping heads on stilts. After heads have been bisque-fired, shape lump of clay about 1 1/2″ square × 3/4″ thick; fit this lump inside the basket, making necessary adjustments. With lump still in basket, press heads gently into lump, forming indentations that will hold the heads in place in the basket; make sure heads are in their final position, allowing for a pillow about 1/4″ thick behind them. Remove heads and lump carefully from basket, separate heads from lump, and coat heads with overglaze. Fire all three pieces to required cone. Using brown watercolor paint, dot brown eyes in indentations, then carefully shellac to make eyes indelible.

Carriage: Remove handle from basket; cut into one 4″ length and two 1 1/2″ lengths. (Or use bristol board; make strips about 3/16″ wide.) Following *Carriage Handle Assembly Diagram,* slip ends of 4″ length through slats of basket, forming the handle. Slip 1 1/2″ lengths through slats; glue to center top of handle. Although handle appears to point straight up in diagram, it should slant away from basket, following the contours of the basket.

For axles, cut two 1 5/8″ lengths of 1/8″-diameter dowel. Paint carriage and dowels white. Cut four wheels, each 3/16″ thick, from 7/8″-diameter dowel; sand with medium, then fine sandpaper. Paint treads red; paint each side of wheel rose; paint circle of white dots on one side of each wheel. Center and glue axles between wheels on plain rose sides of each. Glue axles to base of basket to align with handle. Shellac entire carriage; let dry thoroughly.

Blanket and Pillow: For blanket, cut 4″-diameter circle from fabric; fold in half with right

sides out and edges even. Sew ruffled lace trim across blanket so it extends slightly beyond folded edge. For pillow, cut a 2 1/4 × 2 1/2″ piece of fabric. Fold in half with wrong sides facing, matching 2 1/4″ edges. Sew along two sides, making 1/4″ seam; clip corners, turn to right side, and stuff with fiberfill. Fold raw edges 1/4″ inside; slip-stitch closed.

Assembly: Glue lump of porcelain inside carriage on base with indentations facing up. Glue pillow on top of lump and to handles; see photograph for position. Glue babies' heads so that they rest on pillow over indentations. Tuck blanket around babies with lace edge at their throats; add fiberfill beneath blanket so that it mounds softly. Glue raw edges of blanket inside carriage.

Wrap wire twice around center of handle, twisting ends together. Thread cord through wire; knot ends together for hanging loop. Tie pink ribbon into a bow; glue over wire at top of handle.

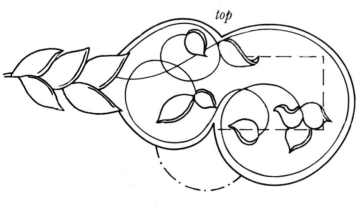

top

CHARIOT SIDE

front wheel

back wheel

GOLDEN SWAN
CHARIOT

Skill Level: Advanced.

Materials: Oven-bake modeling compound. Tracing paper. Hat pin. Orange stick. Knife. Scraps of 14-mesh-to-the-inch mono needlepoint canvas. Thread. Sewing needle. Fiberfill. Bristol board. X-acto knife. Scissors. Pearl cotton, # 5. White glue. Toothpicks. Chains of metal beads (as from keychains). Gold metallic thread. Medallions from paper doilies, various sizes. Silk flowers and leaves. Gold metallic spray paint.

Directions: Trace wing pattern. Make two wing templates from oven-bake modeling compound as follows: Roll compound to 3/8″ thickness. Place wing pattern on compound and transfer heavy lines by pricking through paper into clay with hat pin. Turn tracing paper over, reversing design, and transfer second wing in same manner. Use knife to cut out each template around outer

SCULPTING DIAGRAMS

WING

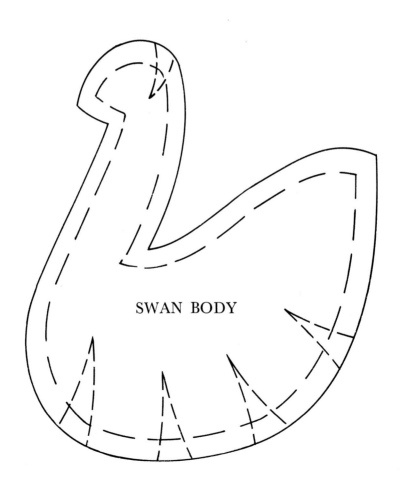

SWAN BODY

edges; then, using orange stick, remove 1/8–1/4″ of clay from within outlines of wings. Scribe feather lines deeply with hat pin. Bake templates in a 325° F. oven until firm.

While templates are baking, use pattern to cut two swan shapes from needlepoint canvas. Make darts in each body by folding and stitching firmly, so that body pieces will become rounded; be sure to reverse shaping for second body piece. Fold seam allowances to wrong side, clipping where necessary. With wrong sides facing, place body pieces together, matching edges and darts; whipstitch together all around, adding stuffing as you go until swan is firmly packed. Cover swan with a thin layer of compound.

When wing templates have cooled, make wings by pressing compound into template, then peeling each wing out carefully, until you have 15 left and 15 right wings. Starting at the tail, gently press wings on each side of body, moving in layers toward neck. Shape neck, head, beak, and eyes following *Sculpting Diagrams*. Cover neck with small bits of compound and etch small feathers with a hat pin. Add final layer of large wings on each side of body, bending them slightly outward. For chariot side decoration, shape 26 leaves from modeling compound, following pattern and making each leaf quite thin. Bake swan and leaves in 325° F. oven until firm, checking often to prevent scorching.

While pieces are baking, cut two sides, two front wheels, two back wheels, one 1 3/4″-square base, and one 1 3/4 × 3/4″ back from bristol board. Glue pearl cotton to each side piece to form vines and rim edges following pattern; be sure to reverse one chariot side before gluing pearl cotton in place. After leaves have cooled, glue to each side piece following pattern for placement. Glue chains of metal beads to edges of each chariot side; see photograph.

To build chariot, glue back behind base with bottom edges flush, making a 90° angle. Glue chains of metal beads around edges of back; cut and glue three medallions from a doily to back. Following dot/dash line on side pattern, glue back wheels in place. Following dash lines on side pattern, glue assembled base and back between sides. For front wheels, cut a 1 1/2″ length of toothpick; insert through center of each front wheel so toothpick protrudes 1/8″ on each side; glue. Center and glue front wheels beneath swan. Glue leafy section of chariot to each side of swan just behind large wings; see photograph.

Spray swan and chariot with several coats of gold metallic paint, allowing each coat to dry. Glue silk flowers inside chariot. Make reins with gold metallic thread and glue to each side of swan's beak, allowing reins to trail into the flowers. Nest in branches of tree.

LAUSCHA SANTA

NOTE: Before beginning, read General Directions for Ceramics on page 14 for additional materials and directions.

Skill Level: Advanced.

Materials: Pre-wedged porcelain clay that fires to cone 06. Loop. Fiberfill. Trowel. Underglaze: red, black. Paintbrushes. Ceramichrome OK Dinnerware Glaze, clear gloss. Ribbon for hanging.

Directions: Although *Side View* depicts complete ornament, this ornament is made in halves; refer to dash lines on *Side View*. Make each ornament half as follows: Referring to *Front View*, fashion a face from porcelain clay, making piece 1 1/4″ thick at nose. Work slowly and carefully, referring to both diagrams to shape rounded figure. Wet the loop or needle if necessary to scribe clean shapes and smooth curves. Use loop to carve out indentations; use needle to incise lines and add definition. When satisfied with front, set aside and work on back. Ornament back is quite plain; shape outline first following *Front View*, then round clay smoothly following *Side View*.

Allow pieces to dry leather hard, then carefully place layer of fiberfill over the front. Turn piece over and place fiberfill and front in the palm of your hand. Using trimming needle and loop, remove excess clay from back, leaving a rounded

cavity in center; be careful not to cut through to the sculpted side. Work very slowly, making walls of ornament about 1/4″ thick; be careful not to press or flatten the sculpted area. Repeat for back of ornament.

Crosshatch edges of each half, apply slip, then gently press halves together. Roll a worm of clay; press on seam and gently trowel into the seam, leaving no demarcation lines.

Roll thick worm of clay into an oval for hanging loop; cut off one side of oval; crosshatch both cut ends. Crosshatch top where oval will be placed; add slip, then gently press oval in place.

It is important that there be at least two openings to the center cavity: this allows air and gases to escape so the form does not explode in the kiln. Allow seams to dry leather hard, then perforate Santa at base and at top behind hanging loop. Allow ornament to become bone dry. When sure ornament is bone dry, fire to cone o6. Paint with black and red underglaze following photograph. Fire to required cone. Paint with overglaze, clean hanging loop, and hang on rod in kiln to fire. Fire to required cone.

Thread hanging loop with 7″ length of ribbon; tie ends together.

SIDE VIEW   FRONT VIEW

WAX ANGEL

Skill Level: Intermediate.

Materials: Oven-bake modeling compound. Medium-weight wire. Hat pin. Acrylic paints: yellow ochre, Prussian blue, white, orange, black, pink. Metallic gold paint. White glue. Thread for hanger. Paraffin wax. Double boiler.

Directions: Following actual-size *Sculpting Diagrams*, fashion angel from oven-bake modeling compound, smoothing and shaping body until it takes on natural curves; use hat pin to sculpt toes and fingers. When satisfied with body, add angel's clothes made from compound; arrange "fabric" so it falls in smooth folds as shown.

Trace wing pattern and use to make two wings; cut two pieces of wire and shape following heavy lines on *Wing Wiring Diagram*. Wrap modeling compound around wire and shape for two wings; use hat pin to incise feathers as shown in *Wing Sculpting Diagram*. Bend wings so they curve; see photograph and diagrams. Bend and insert wire ends from wings into back of finished angel. Bake in 325° F. oven for 20–25 minutes, checking often to prevent scorching. Allow to cool.

Paint wings gold. Mix white and orange acrylics and paint angel flesh. Paint hair and features yellow ochre; paint black eyes and pink mouth. Paint clothes blue. When paint is dry, make hanging loop from thread and insert into back of head below hair using hat pin; glue. While glue is drying, melt wax in double boiler. Dip finished angel in melted wax; hang and allow to cool.

SCULPTING DIAGRAMS

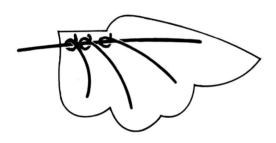

WING WIRING
DIAGRAM

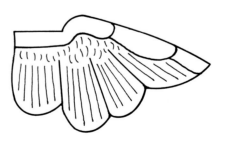

WING SCULPTING
DIAGRAM

The American Catalogue Tree

The American Catalogue Tree has the elusive familiarity of an old photograph of an ancestor. Just as we recognize ourselves in our forebear's features—the shape of the nose, perhaps, or the high forehead—so the American Catalogue Tree seems to be a not-too-distant relative of the contemporary decorated tree. It is a floor-to-ceiling evergreen and marks the first time that full-size firs were popular in this country. Some of its ornaments, too, look familiar: the glass balls and icicles and the garlands of spiky tinsel or gold beads draped from bough to bough.

Yet the tree doesn't have the same feel that today's has: there is something soft, light, and delicate about it. Perhaps the ornaments themselves create this sensation—the spun-glass wings of the angels, fine as gossamer, which make each figure seem to float above the branch beneath it, or the demure cardboard shoes, each one lined with a tiny drawstring silk bag filled with candy. Like the old photograph, the tree seems to hover just outside our reach, forever poised in some sepia-toned moment between then and now.

Part of the tree's allure lies in its sheer variety of ornaments. In the late nineteenth century, when the American Catalogue Tree became popular, ornaments were bought singly or in pairs, not in boxes of a dozen or more as they are today. As the name of the tree implies, the decorations were often purchased from the catalogues of toy importers and from stores such as F. W. Woolworth and Sears, Roebuck, which were then in their infancy. Frank Woolworth, in fact, owned but one store at the time. It was in Lancaster, Pennsylvania, and in later years, when his five-and-dime stores had made him a millionaire many times over, he recounted an entertaining anecdote about a Christmas tree ornament that at the time hadn't been around long, either—the glass Christmas ball.

In the fall of 1880, Woolworth visited a toy importer in Philadelphia to stock up on wares for the coming Christmas. The importer brought out numerous colored glass ornaments, which Woolworth had never seen before. Woolworth wasn't impressed with them. He thought the ornaments would probably break before they ever reached the counter of his store and, even if they didn't, would never sell. However, when the importer guaranteed that Woolworth would sell at least $25 worth, he reluctantly agreed to take a consignment.

"The goods arrived a few days before Christmas," he later recalled, "and, with a great deal of indifference, I put them on my counters. In two days they were gone, and I woke up. But it was too late to order any more, and I had to turn away a big demand. The next Christmas season I was on hand early with what I considered a large order, but it was not large enough. They proved to be the best sellers in my store for the holidays."

Many of these glass ornaments which proved so popular were probably made in Lauscha, Germany. By 1890, glassblowers there had perfected the art of blowing glass ornaments, and some of the most inventive—and difficult to make—examples of the glassblower's art hung on the American Catalogue Tree. Lyres, butterfly bodies with silk wings, tiny trumpets, and vases with arabesque handles were perhaps the finest of these because they were free blown, that is, they were created by pushing and pulling a blob of molten glass into the desired shape, and not by using a

mold. Other popular glass decorations included various fantastic-looking ships draped with crinkly wire and a small sailboat that scudded over a half-moon sea. Lauscha ornaments of balloons and zeppelins reflected the period's fascination with lighter-than-air craft.

Despite their popularity, these glass ornaments didn't occupy as prominent a place on the American Catalogue Tree as they do on today's tree. At least as popular were cotton-batting figures of Santa Claus, angels, and snow fairies, which were also imported from southern Germany. These handmade figures were produced by wrapping thin layers of cotton batting around cardboard forms and embellishing them with glossy, printed faces, buttons, or in the case of angels, gold paper wings. Then a thin layer of glue was spread over the figure, which was frosted with tiny glass particles. The effect was charming: the cotton-batting Santa looked as though he were outfitted in billows of white mink or, perhaps more appropriate, clothed in a snowdrift. German ornament makers in the town of Sebnitz, near Dresden, produced another version of the cotton-batting figure by covering it with webs of delicate, rippling wire to create small boats, sleighs, and cottages that seemed to be draped in curlicued streamers.

Although magazines in the 1870s and 1880s carried complicated designs for do-it-yourself cardboard figures, it wasn't long before dozens of dainty, intricately decorated cardboard ornaments began turning up in stores. Gilded birdcages and ornately decorated Victorian houses, for example, were sold as candy holders. The Victorian house was a marvel of miniature detail: it was two inches high; had four gables made of embossed cardboard and frilly eaves of candy-box lace; and stood on a round platform that held a trove of Christmas candy. Tempting too were little drums with alternating triangles of red and green running around them; miniature tambourines whose faces were decorated with Dutch scenes, such as a windmill on a lake, or elaborate floral still lifes; tiny banjos, mandolins, and other stringed instruments sporting bouquets of rich red roses; a cat sitting contentedly with its paws tucked underneath it; and a jaunty ocean liner with tiny puffs of cotton smoke issuing from its smokestack.

One of the great novelties hanging on the American Catalogue Tree was the papier-mâché fish. This was the Trojan Horse of Christmas ornaments: its interior was hollow, and when the trap door in its side was opened, a cascade of Christmas candy spilled out. Anywhere from six to fifteen inches long, the paper-mâché fish was the brainchild of German craftsmen who had found a way to cover the papier-mâché with a plasterlike substance especially suitable for detailed painting and decorating.

The hallmarks of the American Catalogue Tree, however, were the chromolithographic pictures that fluttered from its branches, perhaps the first Christmas fad in history. Invented in England around 1830, chromolithography replaced hand-tinting and, for the first time, made color pictures inexpensive to produce. In the years after the Civil War, pasting fancy chromolithographic pictures, or "scraps," into books was almost a national pastime in America. Most pictures today are printed in four colors, but in the early days of chromolithography as many as seventeen colors were used, each requiring a separate printing. As a finishing touch, printers embossed certain details to make them stand out and give the picture a three-dimensional appearance.

Scraps quickly found their way onto the Christmas tree. Traditional Christmas figures such as Santa Claus, angels garbed in long, flowing gowns, and pudgy cherubs were especially popular, although most people also gave free rein to their Christmas imagination and used almost any scrap that struck their fancy. By the end of the century, German printers had begun producing chromolithographic figures especially for the tree. These were printed on both sides and pasted together so that, unlike scraps cut from magazines, the desired image always faced outward from the tree. Scraps were also combined with spun-glass ornaments, which were made of fine strands of glass arranged in geometric shapes. Colorful two-masted schooners sailed on spun-glass seas shaped like half moons, and an angel's bright countenance looked out from the center of a spun-glass flower. Even the Lauscha glass balls had chromolithographic scraps affixed to them.

One of our most familiar ornaments, tinsel, or lamé as it was originally called, was still a novelty in the late nineteenth century. The technique for making tinsel, originally used to decorate military uniforms, was developed by the French and copied by German craftsmen as early as the 1600s. The process involved pulling a silver-plated copper wire through several diamond dies until it was reduced to the thickness of a human hair. It was then flattened and twisted around cording to produce a spiky-looking garland, much like silvered pine needles, and bent into all sorts of shapes: six-pointed stars, hearts, wreaths, pretzels, and teardrops, to name just a few. It was also twisted to form an ornate frame or a sinuous brocade that turned an ordinary scrap into a rather original-looking decoration. Today these are among the rarest of antique Christmas ornaments.

Besides tinsel, strings of glass beads imported from Czechoslovakia were also used as garlands for the tree. The glass beads were lightweight and shone like mirrors, the perfect companion for the gelatin lanterns that bathed the tree in soft hues of red, green, and blue. Introduced in 1893, gelatin lanterns were the nineteenth-century's version of the colored Christmas tree light. They were essentially small brass foil boxes backed with pieces of colored gelatin. The sides were perforated, and a candle stood in the middle of the box, which was clamped to a branch or hung by a small chain.

The top of the tree received special attention. It had always been customary to crown the tree with a star, which symbolized the one that guided the Three Wise Men to the manger in Bethlehem. In the 1890s, however, people began topping off the tree with chromolithographs of angels pasted to pieces of cardboard and surrounded by a spiky tinsel frame, or by puffs of lametta, a very fine silver-plated copper wire. German glassblowers skillfully created a tree top from a series of graduated glass balls with reflecting surfaces inside. Each ornament was blown from a single blob of molten glass, a technique that required every ounce of the glassblower's skill.

The American Catalogue Tree marks a milestone in the way in which Christmas was celebrated in this country. Edible ornaments were giving way to decorations that were kept from year to year, and the holiday itself was more commercial than it had ever been before, although hardly so in comparison to today. But the biggest change was the tree itself. An immigrant to these shores only seventy-five years before, it had become the centerpiece of Christmas.

COTTON-BATTING SANTA

Skill Level: Elementary.

Materials: Batting. Black felt. Black and white thread. Sewing needle. Brown watercolor paint. Three gold jewelry findings, 5/8″ diameter. White glue. Chromolithographic print of Santa's face and beard (facial area should measure about 1/4″ from chin to forehead, and 7/8″ wide; if not, adjust all other measurements accordingly). Green florist's wire, 6 1/2″ length. Green florist's tape. Green pearl cotton, # 3. Red seed beads.

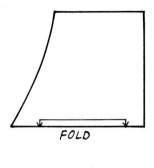

BOOT

Directions: Use pattern to cut two boot pieces from black felt. Fold in half, then whipstitch together along each edge; stuff with fiberfill. For legs, roll a 6″ length of batting and cut to make two cylinders 1 1/4″ diameter × 3″ long; whipstitch long edges in place, then whipstitch boots to bottom of each leg.

For coat, cut batting 10 × 6″. With 10″ measurement as width, position legs next to one another with toes pointing upward along right edge of batting; allow boots to extend just beyond edge of coat. Roll batting around legs, ending with edge over one leg; whipstitch in place. Glue three jewelry findings along stitched edge of batting, with centers of findings 1″, 2 1/2″, and 3 1/2″ above bottom of coat.

For each arm, roll a 6″ length of batting to make a 1″-diameter cylinder. Whipstitch long edges in place. Cut one 2 × 3″ cuff, half the thickness of the rest of the batting; paint with brown watercolor paint. When dry, wrap around center of arm cylinder; whipstitch in place.

Roll ball of batting, making a 2 1/2″-diameter head; paint brown. Press chromolithographic face into one side of ball and glue so there is a border of brown fur around face. Whipstitch head to body, then whipstitch ends of arms to shoulders at each side of head.

Fashion a bag of "goodies" from batting, making bag about 3″ diameter × 3″ long; pull one corner of batting for top of bag, and arrange pulled end over one shoulder with remainder of bag hanging over back; see photograph. Slip-stitch pulled end of bag to hand, and remainder of bag to back.

For tree, fold 6 1/2″ length of wire in half. Cut about thirty 2″ strands of green pearl cotton. Beginning at fold, position one strand centered on wire, then twist other half of wire around strand to secure. Continue placing strands on wire, flush with one another, and securing with a twist of the other end of wire. When strands are all secured, twist wires together at bottom, then wrap tightly with florist's tape. Glue seed beads to tree; trim strands of pearl cotton to graduated lengths to simulate branches. Stroke branches upward with your fingers, then insert tree securely through Santa's hand. Hang with thread inserted through top of hat.

Harlequin Drum

Windmill Drum

WINDMILL AND HARLEQUIN DRUMS

NOTE: Before beginning, read General Directions for Transferring Designs on page 14.

Skill Level: Intermediate.

Materials: *For Each:* White oaktag, 8 × 10″. Watercolor paper, 400 lb. bond. Compass. Scissors. Mat knife. Ruler. Watercolor paints. Fine paintbrushes. Gold elastic thread. Aluminum foil. Gold beading wire, #34. White glue. Fine sandpaper. *For Windmill Drum:* Gold braid trim 3/8″ wide, 3/4 yard. Four jingle bells. *For Harlequin Drum:* Embossed gold foil trim 3/8″ wide, 7 1/4″ length. Yellow soutache braid.

Directions: *For Each Drum:* Use compass to draw two circles on watercolor paper following individual directions for diameter. Draw rectangle on oaktag following dimensions given. Next, cut two strips of oaktag, each 1/4″ wide and 1/8″ shorter than the width (longer measurement) of rectangle.

On wrong side of rectangle, draw lines 1/4″ and 1/2″ away from each long edge (a total of four lines drawn). With edges flush at one short end, glue strips to rectangle between marked lines (see *Assembly Diagram*); let dry. Following individual directions, decorate rectangle and paint top and bottom with watercolor paints

WINDMILL DRUM

and colored pencils. With decorative side facing out, roll rectangle into a tube and glue, lapping plain edge of tube 1/8″ over edge with glued strips; this will reduce bulk. Hold tube securely until glue dries. Add additional details and hanger, then insert and glue circles into drum with painted sides out, resting each circle on oaktag "shelf."

Windmill Drum: Diameter of circle: 3″. Rectangle: 2 1/4 × 9 5/8″. Trace pattern, including outline; transfer twice to water-color paper. Transfer side motif design to rectangle, repeating as many times as necessary to fit evenly. Paint side using water-color paints as follows: paint background mauve; paint outlined areas gray; paint dark areas black. For top and bottom, paint background of windmill design in shades of pink, mauve, and sepia as shown in photo-graph; paint all dark areas black.

To decorate side, cut two 9 5/8″ lengths of gold braid. Glue around tube, flush with outer edges; lap ends neatly over one another. Mark off four positions around tube, one each centered at 12, 3, 6, and 9 o'clock. Cut four 1″ lengths of gold beading wire. Curve each wire into a small U. Thread one through each jingle bell, then insert into oaktag at a marked position, bending wire outward inside tube to secure bell in place. Attach loop of wire to one jingle bell for hanging. Insert and glue top and bottom in place, positioning each so top of windmill design (labeled X in diagram) is even with top jingle bell.

Harlequin Drum: Diameter of circle: 2 1/4″. Rectangle: 1 1/2 × 7 1/4″. For side, trace and complete half pattern, in-dicated by dash line. Transfer pattern to rectangle; plain 1/8″ strip is for overlap and should occur at only one edge. Using watercolor paints, paint center stripe of side purple; paint two narrow stripes lavender; paint inner triangles kelly green; paint outer triangles red. For top and bottom, paint with a wash of sepia and pale pink.

To decorate side, glue 7 1/4″ length of gold embossed paper around side in center of purple stripe; lap ends neatly over one another. Cut 1″ length of gold beading wire; fold in half, forming a loop, and twist ends together. Insert ends into side of drum; bend wire ends out-ward inside drum to secure loop. Thread soutache braid through wire loop and tie for hanger. Insert top and bottom into drum. Glue gold elastic thread around top and bottom edges.

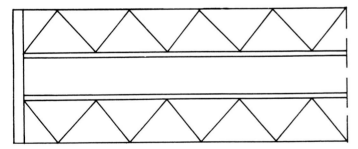

HARLEQUIN DRUM SIDE

WINDMILL DRUM SIDE

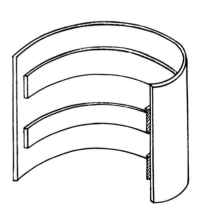

ASSEMBLY DIAGRAM

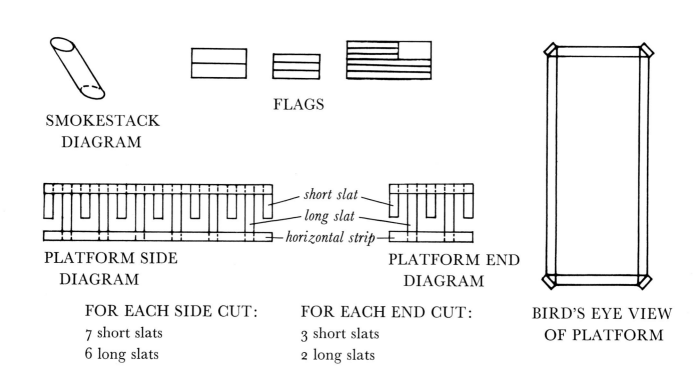

SMOKESTACK
DIAGRAM

FLAGS

PLATFORM SIDE
DIAGRAM

short slat
long slat
horizontal strip

PLATFORM END
DIAGRAM

BIRD'S EYE VIEW
OF PLATFORM

FOR EACH SIDE CUT:
7 short slats
6 long slats
3 horizontal strips

FOR EACH END CUT:
3 short slats
2 long slats
3 horizontal strips

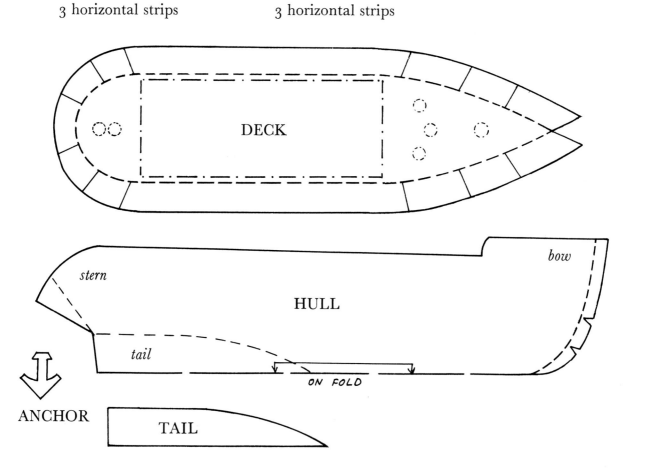

DECK

bow

stern

HULL

tail

ON FOLD

ANCHOR

TAIL

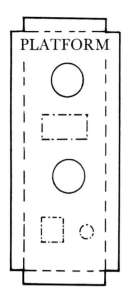

STEAMSHIP

NOTE: Before beginning, read General Directions for Transferring Designs on page 14.

Skill Level: Advanced.

Materials: Watercolor paper, 50 lb. bond. Scrap of cardboard, 1/8″ thick. Mat board, 1/16″ thick. Brown paper. Scissors. X-acto knife. Metal-edge ruler. Blunt-tipped darning needle. Craft glue that bonds quickly. Metallic gold trim, 3/8″ wide. Metallic gold paper medallions: one 3/8″ diameter, two 5/8″ diameter. Acrylic paints: red, black, cream, brown. Colored pencils: red, blue, yellow, green, orange. Gray watercolor paint. Paintbrush. Polyester fiberfill. Scraps of 14-mesh-to-the-inch mono needlepoint canvas. Gold pearl cotton, #3. Fine gold wire for hanging.

Directions: Trace patterns. Transfer the following to watercolor paper: one hull, placing long dash line on fold of paper; one deck; one platform; three different flags. Use ruler to draw one 5/8 × 12″ strip. Transfer one tail to 1/8″-thick cardboard. Cut out all pieces on solid lines, carefully cutting out two holes in platform where indicated. To make bending easier, trace along all fold lines (dash lines) with blunt-tipped darning needle. All dot/dash lines are placement lines.

For hull of ship, fold along long dash line, then fold bow and stern edges along short dash lines and glue together, lapping triangular-shaped pieces at stern over one another, and gluing clipped bow edges together *inside* hull. Insert cardboard tail inside ship at stern and glue in place, pressing and folding hull to tail until glue is dry. Using acrylics, paint hull

bright red; paint one side of 5/8 × 12″ strip black; paint deck and platform cream with streaks of brown to resemble wood grain.

When paint is dry, wrap black strip around hull so bottom edge of strip is 7/8″ above base of ship; glue in place, lapping ends over one another at stern. Glue gold metallic trim around hull and black strip so trim is even with top edge of hull, lapping ends as for black strip; for extension at bow, cut an extra strip of gold trim and glue in place. Cut anchor from gold trim using pattern; glue to bow on one side of ship. Glue 5/8″ medallions together with gold sides outward; glue to hull at stern of ship. Clip edges of deck with scissors in positions indicated; fold along short dash lines, then insert and glue deck into hull so top of deck is 1/4″ below top edge of hull.

Following actual-size *Plat-*

137

form Side Diagram and *Platform End Diagram*, cut and assemble mat board pieces to make two sides and two ends. (*Note:* Always work with white side of mat board facing outward; use X-acto knife against metal-edge ruler for straight, accurate cuts.) Glue extra horizontal strip to wrong side of each piece, even with bottom edge of short slats. From mat board, also cut four corner pieces, each 1/8 × 5/8"; cut one 1/4 × 1/2" hatch and one 1/4"-square hatch and set aside. Following *Bird's Eye View*, assemble sides and ends of platform, and glue corner strips in place. Fold platform along fine dash lines and insert into side/end assembly; glue so platform is about 1/8" below sides and ends. Paint one side and all cut edges of each hatch black; glue to platform in positions indicated by dot/dash lines. Glue platform assembly to deck following dot/dash lines on pattern.

From brown paper, cut two 1 3/8 × 2" pieces for smokestacks. Roll and glue each piece of paper, making two tubes 1 3/8" long and about 3/8" in diameter. Bevel ends of smokestacks following *Smokestack Diagram*, then insert into holes of platform and glue with beveled edge resting on deck and smokestacks angled toward stern; see photograph. Glue 3/8" medallion to deck at stern.

Roll a 5 1/2" length of brown paper into a 1/8"-diameter tube; glue. Cut tube into two 1 3/4" masts and two 1" poles. Glue masts centered on deck in

front and back of platform. Glue one 1" pole to center of stern medallion and one near point of bow. (Check dot/dash lines on deck pattern for exact placement.) Roll a 1 1/8" length of brown paper into a 1/8"-diameter tube; cut into three 3/8" lengths for vent ducts. Bend top 1/8" of each tube over and paint red. Following pattern and photograph, glue straight ends to each side of deck in front of platform; glue one to platform next to hatch.

Using colored pencils, color one American flag, one green/white flag, and one yellow flag with an orange center stripe. Bend flags slightly so they appear to be blowing in the wind, then glue to tops of masts and stern pole; position all flags so they are "blowing" toward the stern.

For rope ladders, cut three strips of needlepoint canvas, each 2" long and two meshes wide; paint each side black. Glue one to bow mast and deck; glue two to stern mast and deck; see photograph. Cut three lengths of gold pearl cotton for ropes. Drag through glue and glue two ropes from tip of bow to top of bow mast; glue one rope from deck at stern mast to top of stern mast. For smoke, shape two fluffs of fiberfill; paint with gray watercolor paint. Glue one inside each smokestack.

Cut two 10" lengths of fine gold wire. Attach one end to each corner of platform; twist together at top for hanging loop.

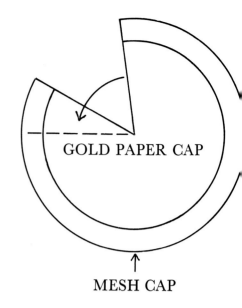

GOLD PAPER CAP

MESH CAP

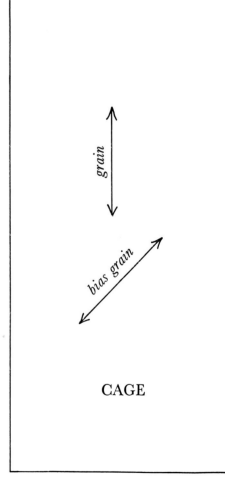

grain

bias grain

CAGE

TWO GILDED BIRDCAGES

Skill Level: Intermediate.

Materials: Scraps of 14-mesh-to-the-inch mono needlepoint canvas. Lightweight cardboard. Compass. White glue. Scissors. Sewing needle. Gold metallic thread. Fine gold wire. Gold paint. Paintbrush. Gold jewelry findings with hanging loop or central hole. Seed beads. Gold sequins. Pearl cotton, #3. Aluminum foil. Gold wrapping paper and gold scalloped filigree paper. 1/4" wide trim: looped braid or satin ribbon.

1/8" wide trim: rickrack or satin ribbon.

Directions: Use pattern to cut out cage from needlepoint canvas, following one of the grain lines. Use compass to draw 1 1/2" circle on lightweight cardboard; cut out. Make 1/8" clips in cardboard all around edge; bend clipped edges up, all in the same direction. Roll canvas into a tube; glue 2 1/2" edges together, lapping canvas 1/4" over itself. When glue dries, insert clipped edge of cardboard circle into one end of tube and glue in place, clipping cardboard a little deeper if necessary to make circle fit.

To make gold paper cap, use

inner line of pattern to cut one cap from lightweight cardboard. Roll into conical shape; lap and glue edges together following arrow and dash lines. Cover cap with gold wrapping paper, trimming paper to fit smoothly and evenly. Glue gold filigree trim around edges of cap. Glue jewelry finding to top of cap.

For mesh cap, cut cap from lightweight cardboard following outer line of pattern; lap and glue as described above, then cover neatly with aluminum foil. Cut 23 lengths of pearl cotton, each 1 1/4" long. Pour small amount of white glue into a bowl or cup and drag each length of pearl cotton through the glue. After strand has been covered with glue, drape it on aluminum-covered cap, so one end is at peak and the other end is extending straight downward. Continue adding all 23 lengths of cotton to cap in this manner. Cut three 6 1/2" lengths of pearl cotton to wrap around glued strands. Drag in glue, then wrap one around bottom, the second 1/2" above bottom, and the third 3/4" above bottom, trimming as necessary to fit. Glue jewelry finding to top, covering ends of strands. Let glue dry, then carefully remove from aluminum-covered cap. Glue braid trim around bottom edge of cap.

Decorate cages as follows: Glue braid or 1/4" satin ribbon around bottom edge. Glue rickrack or 1/8" satin ribbon 3/4" and 1 1/4" above bottom of cage, trimming to fit and lapping ends neatly over one another. Using paintbrush and gold paint, paint cage, bottom, trimmings, and mesh top; there is no need to paint the gold paper cap.

If using jewelry finding with hanging loop, wire cap to cage with fine gold wire, then attach gold thread to loop for hanger. If using jewelry finding with center hole and no hanging loop, thread sewing needle with gold metallic thread and knot one end. Insert needle through one seed bead and one gold sequin, then through center of bottom of cage. Run thread up through the cage, and through the cap and jewelry finding; make a loop with the thread for hanging, then knot and clip away excess thread.

MANDOLIN

NOTE: *Before beginning, read General Directions for Transferring Designs on page 14.*

Skill Level: Intermediate.

Materials: White oaktag, 8 × 10″. Watercolor paper, 400 lb. bond. Scissors. Mat knife. Ruler. White glue. Aluminum foil. Fine sandpaper. Watercolor paints. Gold metallic paint. Fine paintbrushes. Colored pencils. Sewing needle with large eye. Gold elastic thread. Sequin pins.

Directions: Trace patterns for front (including outline), top, center, and side motifs. Transfer the following to watercolor

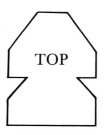

TOP

CENTER

SIDE MOTIFS

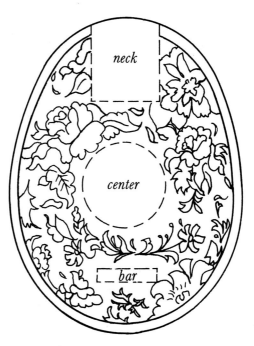

MANDOLIN FRONT

140

paper: one entire front pattern, one front outline only (for back), one center, two tops, two 3/4 × 3″ neck pieces, and one 1/8 × 5/8″ bar. On oaktag, draw one 3/4 × 8 3/4″ rectangular strip for side; transfer floral motifs for side to strip, alternating motifs evenly along length. Cut out all pieces using scissors and mat knife.

For neck, paint one side of each piece with white glue; press together from center outward with edges even, wiping away excess glue as necessary. Sand edges with fine sandpaper until smooth and even. Place between two pieces of aluminum foil and let dry under heavy weight for 24 hours.

While waiting for neck to dry, paint the following metallic gold: one side of back, extending color for 1/2″ onto other side; both sides of each top; outer edges of center and front, extending color for 1/2″ onto other side of front. Cover entire front with an ivory wash background. Then, using watercolor paints and colored pencils, paint front with a variety of colors; see photograph for ideas. Paint side first with an ivory wash, then with red flowers and lime green leaves. Paint middle of center red. Paint bar, including edges, black. When dry, paint sanded edges and one side of neck black; paint other side metallic gold. Paint thin gold stripes on black side of neck for frets, making stripes 1/8″ apart; extend stripes over side edges.

To assemble, roll rectangle into a ring with painted side out

and glue, lapping ends 1/4″ over one another; hold securely until dry. Glue tube to wrong side of back, adjusting tube to fit oval shape; let dry thoroughly. Glue neck, center, and bottom bar to front in positions indicated by dash lines on diagram. Cut five 5 1/2″ lengths of gold elastic thread. Secure ends to front, one at a time, as follows: Thread elastic end through sewing needle; insert needle through front just above bar and draw 1/2″ of elastic to wrong side; remove

needle; knot thread. Repeat for other four lengths of elastic, spacing them evenly across the bar. On right side, insert one sequin pin through front at end of each strand. Run strands directly up to top of neck, gluing ends at top so they are spaced evenly; trim away any excess elastic. Sandwich top end of neck between two top pieces; glue together securely. Glue front to side same as for back. Cut 12″ length of gold elastic; knot ends and attach to top for hanging loop.

CHROMOLITHO-GRAPHIC PRINT ON LAUSCHA GLASS BALL

Skill Level: Elementary.

Materials: Glass ball. Two chromolithographic prints in size compatible to ball. Gold jewelry finding. Wire hanging loop. Gold braid trim. White glue. Damp cloth. Curved cuticle scissors.

Directions: Using curved cuticle scissors, cut out chromolithographic motifs. Glue motif to each side of ball as follows: Spread meager amount of glue on wrong side of print; press carefully onto ornament, wiping away excess glue with damp cloth as you press. Cut gold braid trim to fit around ball; glue as for print. Glue jewelry finding to top of ball. Insert hanging loop inside center of jewelry finding.

CORNUCOPIA

Skill Level: Elementary.

Materials: Lightweight cardboard. Wrapping paper. Scissors. Spray adhesive. Chromolithographic print. Curved cuticle scissors. Cotton print fabric, 3 × 19″. Matching thread. Gold pearl cotton, # 3. White glue. Gold braid trim with tiny fringe.

142

Directions: Use pattern to cut one cone each from lightweight cardboard and wrapping paper. Using spray adhesive, glue wrapping paper smoothly to cardboard. With decorative side out, overlap and glue edges of cone together, holding securely until glue dries. Using curved cuticle scissors, carefully cut out chromolithographic print; spray wrong side of print with adhesive and glue to cone on side opposite seam.

Stitch 1/4″ hem along both short edges of fabric; make a 3/8″ casing along one long edge of fabric; machine-baste across opposite long edge. Cut 32″ length of pearl cotton; thread through casing. Tie ends together, then bury knot inside casing. Gather basted edge of fabric to fit inside cone; glue raw edge of fabric inside cone as shown in photograph, lapping short edges of fabric over one another at seam of cone. Glue braid trim around top edge of cone. Make a tiny slit in upper edge of fabric casing opposite short lapped edges; pull pearl cotton out through opening and gather top edge of fabric evenly between pearl cotton loops.

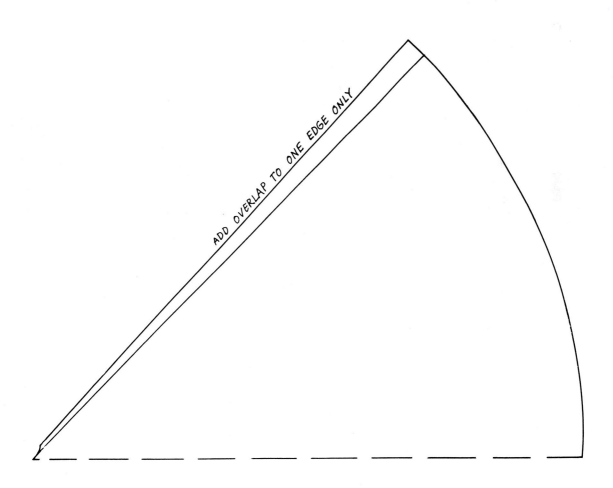

ADD OVERLAP TO ONE EDGE ONLY

The Electric Tree

Just as it changed the face of America, the invention of the electric light bulb forever altered the appearance of the decorated tree. Today we take electric Christmas lights for granted. Once a tree has been set up, the lights are usually the first ornaments to be put on it, and they provide the foundation for the tinsel and glitter to follow. But it was only seventy years ago that some 12,000 people crowded into Madison Square Park in New York City to see the then-novel spectacle of a tall, stately fir twinkling with colored lights.

Although they didn't know it, those New Yorkers were witnessing a revolution in Christmas decorations. For more than four hundred years the candle had been the most important decoration on the tree. Lit candles created a hushed, almost primitive aura and, because of their long history as a religious symbol, conveyed a deep spiritual meaning as well.

Unfortunately they also set homes ablaze with alarming frequency. Each December newspapers were filled with horrific stories of fires that started when a candle fell or was knocked off a Christmas tree. Still, no one could resist the candle's bewitching glow, and more than a few inventors tried unsuccessfully to come up with a safe way to celebrate Christmas by candlelight. One English firm even manufactured a cast-iron Christmas tree illuminated by gas jets. It was called "The Improved German Christmas Tree," and not surprisingly it never caught on.

The electric Christmas tree light seemed to be the answer to the problem. It was an early offshoot of the incandescent bulb invented by Thomas Edison in 1879. The first Christmas tree lights ever made were blown in Edison's laboratory at Menlo Park, New Jersey, and placed on the tree of Edward Johnson, a vice-president of the Edison Electric Company, in 1910. Because they were expensive, Christmas lights were at first popular only among the wealthy, who often gave parties to show off their new electric trees. It wasn't long, however, before they were mass produced and inexpensive, and by the 1930s, when the America Electric Tree really became popular, the candle had been virtually snuffed out as a Christmas decoration.

The first Christmas lights were rather unimaginative copies of electric bulbs with pieces of crepe paper wrapped around them to provide color. The lively Christmas imaginations of Austrian craftsmen soon changed that, however. Starting in 1909, a small menagerie of handpainted Christmas lights—canaries, dogs, cats, and owls—issued from their workshops for export to America, where they quickly became popular. It had always been customary in Germany and Austria to decorate Christmas trees with fruit and paper flowers, and so the Austrian glassblowers also turned out glass strawberries, pears, and peaches and glass bouquets of lilies and roses. Figures such as clowns, snowmen, and Santa Clauses, of course, were always popular.

It took American manufacturers until the 1920s and 1930s to begin making figurative lights, but when they did, they turned out a host of colorful bulbs that look refreshingly old-fashioned today. There were colored stars, including one whimsical version with a smiling quarter moon on it; a top-hatted dog and a sad-eyed cat outfitted in a red coat and playing a mandolin; red roses and tulips; a sleek-looking zeppelin with an American flag emblazoned on its side; and, of course, a grand, bright, white star to illuminate the top of the tree.

The American Electric Tree continued the trend toward decorating with manufactured ornaments begun in the 1880s. After World War I, American businessmen, realizing that a vast market for Christmas decorations existed, rushed to satisfy it with a dizzying—and in some instances dazzling—array of Christmas ornaments. Christmas lights were just the tip of the iceberg: by the 1920s and 1930s, yesterday's handcarved wooden star had by and large given way to today's manufactured Christmas ball.

There was almost no limit to what could be hung on the American Electric Tree. Ornaments could be traditional, like Santa Clauses cut from crepe paper; exotic, like Japanese paper lanterns, parasols, and fans with lacquered handles; or jazzy and unfamiliar, like the small champagne buckets that appeared on many trees in the 1950s. Twisted-wire ornaments were extremely popular and were so simple to make that one wonders why people bothered buying them. The glittery wire was crinkled and tied to form galaxies of stars and comets with thin silvery tails, rosettes, butterflies, frames to hold tinsel angels, and wreaths.

Although the Depression saw the dissolution of many firms, one manufacturer combined the entrepreneurial and Christmas spirits to produce some of the most popular, and inexpensive, ornaments of the time. These were brightly colored pieces of cardboard sprinkled with clear, shiny crystals, and they were manufactured in the shape of little wagons, baby carriages, toy drums, and houses, which could be combined under the tree to form a small village.

Fairly tales and American popular culture were also rich sources of inspiration for ornament makers. Snow White and the Seven Dwarfs, Mickey Mouse, Donald Duck, and other Disney characters made their debut on American Christmas trees in the 1930s. Decals of each figure were affixed to small lampshades, which were placed over ordinary Christmas bulbs. At the same time, paper ornaments and lights in the shape of well-known comic book characters like Popeye, Little Orphan Annie, and Dick Tracy also began turning up on trees all over America. The lights were made in Japan, the source of an increasing number of Christmas bulbs in the 1920s and 1930s. American manufacturers had turned to Japan as an alternate source of Christmas lights as a result of their experience in World War I, when products from Europe, up to that time the largest supplier, were cut off.

The Japanese glassblowers and painters were no match for the European craftsmen, however. Their figures were cruder and thicker, and because the paint they used on the bulbs tended to flake, they made their figures from white milk glass, the opacity of which made this defect less apparent. Some of the Japanese figures were and still are quite comical: the blown-glass Santa Claus, for example, looks more like Buddha than jolly Kriss Kringle.

In the 1930s a basement inventor named Carl Otis gave the electric Christmas tree light a new twist. An accountant for Montgomery-Ward, Otis hit upon the idea of filling ordinary Christmas bulbs with methylene chloride, a liquid that bubbles merrily at low temperatures. The peculiar appeal of Bubble-Lites, as Otis christened his invention, was their ability to turn a Christmas tree into a pyramid of boiling colors. Otis's invention was introduced in 1945. Sales were initially slow, but in the 1950s, Bubble-Lites became a national craze. Millions were sold in just a few years, and then, just as suddenly, the Bubble-Lite went the way of the Hula-Hoop.

Despite its large number of manufactured ornaments, the American Electric Tree also reflects the ingenuity people have always displayed at Christmastime for tying, cutting, shaping, and gluing ordinary household objects to produce simple but surprisingly attractive decorations. Ordinary spools of thread, for example, were often decorated with paper cutouts and fastened to the tree with colored cellophane tape, and sticks of chewing gum left in the foil wrappers were hung from branches to glint with the reflection of colored lights. The traditional garland of popcorn and cranberries was updated with Life Saver candies or baking cups strung together with a bright red ribbon. The tree shimmered with reflections created by pocket mirrors painted with brightly colored designs. Choirs of angels were made from packets of conical drinking cups, the kind found at any office water cooler, and an ordinary tin-can lid could be snipped into a star, frosted with glitter, and placed at the top of the tree.

Next to electric lights, Christmas balls were the most frequently seen ornament on the American Electric Tree. Christmas balls had been popular since the late nineteenth century, and until the 1930s, most were handmade and imported from central Europe. Then American importers, realizing another war was imminent in Europe, began looking for a domestic source.

The Corning Glass Works came up with an ingenious method of blowing glass balls by using a machine designed in 1926 to blow light bulbs. The process involved running a ribbon of molten glass over molds at high speed. As the glass was positioned over each mold, a burst of compressed air was blown into the glass to shape it into a sphere. The clear glass ball was then put into a machine called a jiggler. Silver paint was injected into the ball, and the jiggler, by shaking the ball, spread the paint evenly around the inside. The ball was then dipped into lacquer to color it and sent on to another machine which sprayed paint through a silkscreen stencil to create a Christmas design on it. Corning's machine produced more than two thousand Christmas balls per minute, more than an individual craftsman could make in a day, and, surprisingly, the manufactured version turned out to be more durable than the handmade one.

The electric tree has come a long way since the first one was put up in the New York City town house of Edward Johnson; it is certainly a far cry from the simpler, more religious Paradise Tree, its four-hundred-year-old ancestor. And this is not the end of the line. Like all vital expressions of the human spirit, the decorated tree will continue to change. Our delight in it, however, will assuredly remain.

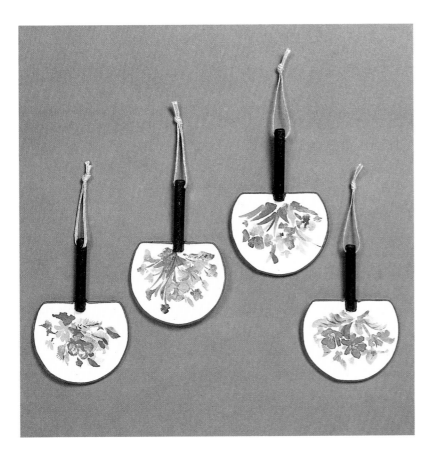

JAPANESE FAN

NOTE: Before beginning, read General Directions for Transferring Designs on page 14.

Skill Level: Elementary.

Materials: Tracing paper. Pencil. Watercolor paper, 400 lb. bond. Watercolor paints: desired colors. Paintbrush. Scissors. White glue. Basswood dowel 1/4″ diameter, 2″ long. Sandpaper. Tack cloth. Drill with 1/8″ bit. X-acto knife. Black acrylic paint. Clear nail polish. Red braid trim 1/8″ wide, 1/4 yard. Silver metallic cord, 6″ length.

Directions: Trace pattern for fan and use to cut one shape from watercolor paper. Using watercolor paints and brush, paint irises, stems, and leaves on paper following pattern, or follow photograph for variations.

For handle, sand ends of dowel until rounded; dust with tack cloth. Make a 3/8″ slice across diameter of one end of dowel using X-acto knife; carefully slice again until watercolor paper fits snugly in groove. At opposite end of dowel drill hole 1/4″ away from end and in same direction as groove. Paint handle black. Coat with layers of clear nail polish until shiny; do not clog groove or hanging hole. Insert base of fan into groove of handle in position indicated by dot/dash lines on pattern; glue. Glue red braid trim around edges of fan. Insert silver cord through hanging hole; knot ends together.

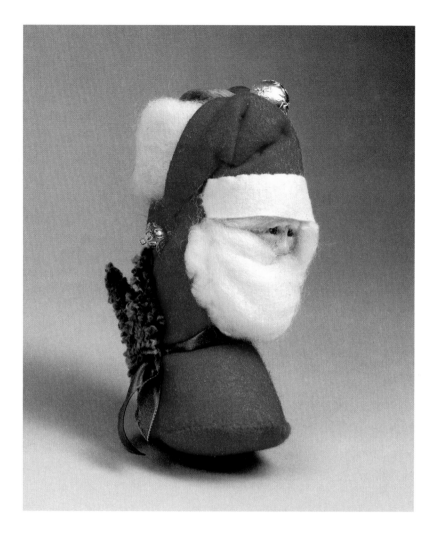

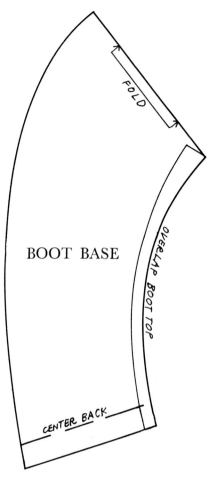

BOOT BASE

FOLD

OVERLAP BOOT TOP

CENTER BACK

SANTA IN BOOT

Skill Level: Intermediate.

Materials: Oven-bake modeling compound. Toothpick. Half of a walnut shell. Acrylic paints: red, white, blue, brown, black. Fine paintbrush. Polyester fiberfill. Scissors. White glue. 14-mesh-to-the-inch mono needlepoint canvas. Red and white felt. Green satin ribbon 3/8″ wide, 1/4 yard. Emerald green pearl cotton, #3. Red sequins. Green florist's wire. Gold filigree bead. Matching thread. Sewing needle. Straight pin.

Directions: Following *Head Sculpting Diagrams*, fashion Santa's head from oven-bake modeling compound wrapped around the walnut half shell; the shell is used as a size reference and can be baked with the modeling compound. Use toothpick and your fingers to carefully form the nose, fat cheeks, chin, and indentations for eyes; it is not necessary to fashion a mouth. When satisfied with head, bake following package directions, then paint flesh by mixing white with pink; add extra red to the cheeks and

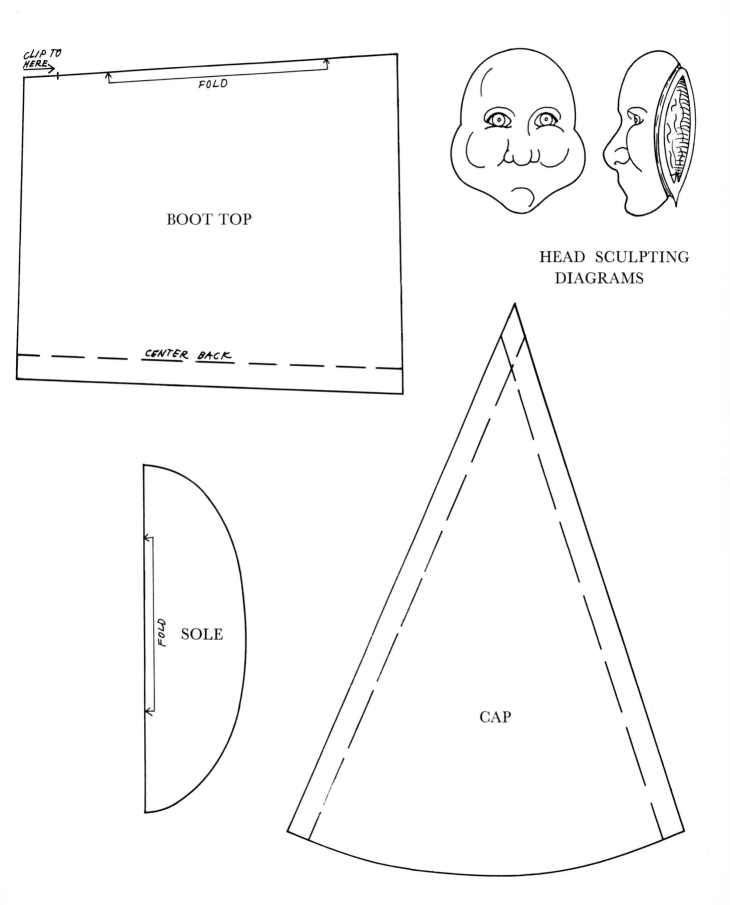

CLIP TO
HERE

FOLD

BOOT TOP

CENTER BACK

HEAD SCULPTING
DIAGRAMS

FOLD

SOLE

CAP

nose. Paint eyes white and blue, with black pupils. Outline eyes with brown; paint tiny brown eyelashes. Wrap and glue fiberfill around head for hair and beard. Cut fluffs of fiberfill for eyebrows; shape and glue just above eyes. For beard, run parallel strands of fiberfill from ear to ear; beard should measure 2″ wide just below nose. For mouth, attach red sequin with a straight pin 1/8″ below nose.

Use pattern to cut one cap from red felt. Stitch long edges together; turn to right side and stuff lightly with fiberfill. Glue bottom edges of cap to head, 3/8″ above eyes; glue edge over walnut shell at back. Set head aside.

Use patterns to cut one boot top, one boot base, and one sole each from needlepoint canvas and red felt. Cut 3/4 × 4″ strip from white felt. Construct needlepoint boot first: For top and base, lap back edges 1/4″ and whipstitch to hold. Insert top inside base following lines on pattern; whipstitch together. Whipstitch sole to base. Wrap felt top around canvas top, lapping edges over one another neatly at back; slip-stitch edge in place, catching portions of the canvas as you stitch. Lap and stitch felt base to canvas in same manner. Whipstitch felt sole to canvas. Stuff base of boot firmly with fiberfill. Wrap and tack fiberfill around top of boot for a 1 1/2″ cuff; extend fiberfill over top of boot to inside, covering raw edges.

Wrap green satin ribbon around boot over joining of top and base; tie into a bow on one side of boot, then slip-stitch each long edge of ribbon in place, covering seam. To make branches, cut one 5″ and two 4″ lengths of florist's wire; fold each in half. Make each branch as follows: Cut 1″-wide lengths of green pearl cotton. Beginning at fold, position one strand, centered, on wire, then twist other half of wire around strand to secure. Continue placing strands on wire, flush with one another, and securing each with a twist of the other end of wire. When all strands are secured to within 1/4″ of bottom, twist wires together at bottom. Trim strands of pearl cotton to graduated lengths (about 1/4″ wide at top to 1″ wide at base). Glue red sequins to each branch at random. Tack branches to boot at bow of ribbon, positioning longest branch in center.

Position Santa's head on opposite side of boot toward the front, so bottom of cap is even with bottom of fiberfill cuff; tack securely in place, bending cap down toward center front of boot as shown in photograph. Position white felt strip over bottom of cap; slip-stitch to boot at each end, and to cap along top edge. Sew gold filigree bead to end of cap. Cut 9″ length of green pearl cotton for hanger; tack inside boot on each side.

WIRED LAUSCHA GLASS ORNAMENTS

Skill Level: Intermediate.

Materials: *For Each:* Glass ball, small (1 1/2″ diameter) or large (2 1/4″ diameter). Fine gold wire. Wire coat hanger. Wire cutters. Metallic gold thread. Two 1/2″-diameter gold jewelry findings with central holes. White glue. *For Small Ornament:* 3/8″-diameter gold jewelry finding. Five pink fabric flowers with yellow centers and wire stems. Eight pearls for stringing, about 1/4″ diameter. *For Large Ornament:* Chromolithographic print of angels. Curved cuticle scissors. Crystal star bead. Brown paper. Gold metallic paint. Two gold beads, about 1/4″ diameter.

Directions: *Technique:* To achieve the twisted wire effect, use wire cutters to cut straight length of wire coat hanger. Wind fine gold wire tightly around straight length of coat hanger. Gently slip off the hanger to retain the coil, then clip to desired length plus about 1/2″ at each end for twisting. Wind twisted wire around ornament following individual directions, then twist ends together and insert into gold jewelry finding or bead to secure, gluing if necessary. *Small Ornament:* Glue 3/8″ jewelry finding over opening in glass ball to cover cut edges; hold ornament while working so jewelry finding is at one side. Cut lengths of twisted wire to fit across ornament from side to side. Position lengths of wire across ornament, securing around jewelry finding at one side and twisting ends together at other side until ornament is enclosed. Give ends a final tight twist to secure, then make tassels as follows: For each side, cut one 4″ strand, one 3″ strand, and two 2″ strands of gold metallic thread. Insert each strand through a pearl, then gather ends of all strands together and insert through 1/2″-diameter jewelry finding; twist and tie to twisted wire ends on each side of ornament. Push jewelry finding toward the wires until both wires and metallic thread are through the center of the finding; glue.

Insert and wrap wire stems of fabric flowers around the twisted wires, making a row of flowers across the top of the ornament. Cut 6″ length of gold metallic thread; tie each end to side of ornament for hanging loop.

Large Ornament: Carefully cut out chromolithographic print using curved cuticle scissors. Cut brown wrapping paper to 5″ length and 15″ width. Roll wrapping paper into 5″-high tube that will fit inside hole of glass ball. When tube is required diameter, trim away excess paper and glue end securely. Paint tube metallic

gold; glue 1/2″ of tube inside ornament. Glue chromolithographic print to tube so base of print rests on ornament. Glue crystal star to tube above print.

Cut lengths of twisted wire to fit vertically on ornament and tube as follows: For base of ornament, insert twisted wire ends through gold bead, then run wire up to top of tube and insert into gold jewelry finding. Enclose ornament and print with twisted wire in this manner; portions of print may protrude beyond wire (see photograph). When satisfied, twist ends together tightly, then glue

finding to top of tube and bead to bottom of ornament, making sure it is centered.

For tassel, cut about twenty-five 4″ lengths of gold metallic thread. Position lengths together on work surface with ends even; tie in center with a length of thread. Smooth strands in one direction, then wrap thread around top to hold. Glue gold jewelry finding to top of tassel. Cut 6″ length of gold metallic thread; insert through loose gold bead and top of jewelry finding, then tie into a loop. Attach loop to base of ornament with fine gold wire.

CHAMPAGNE BOTTLE IN BUCKET

Skill Level: Intermediate.

Materials: Watercolor paper, 40 lb. bond. Ruler. Scissors. Compass. White glue. Flour. Water. Newspaper. Medium-weight wire. Acrylic paints: white, green. Gold foil. Silver sparkling tinsel flakes. Silver braid trim 1/8″ wide, 1/3 yard. Red cord for hanging.

Directions: Use pattern for bucket to cut one piece from watercolor paper. Lap and glue straight edges over one another following line on pattern. Use compass to draw 1 1/4″-diameter circle on watercolor paper for base; cut out. Insert base into bucket through wide opening (top); glue in place at bottom. Use pattern to cut one top from watercolor paper. Cut out interior circle along dash line, then clip into paper following lines on pattern. Bend all clipped edges to one side (wrong side) along solid line. Lap and glue ends of extension over one another following line on pattern so lip extends on right side; on wrong side, glue base of extension to edges of ice. Insert top into bucket and glue with top edges even.

Cut two 1/4 × 1″ strips from paper for side loops; roll and glue each into a 1/4″-diameter tube, then glue to each side of bucket, centered between top and bottom. Shape two wire handles following *Handle Diagram;* glue ends inside loops. Paint entire bucket white, including wire handles.

Using your fingers, brush white glue over exterior of bucket, including loops, and over extensions on interior of bucket; coat liberally with silver flakes. Allow to dry, then gently shake off excess. Glue silver braid trim to exterior of bucket around top and bottom edges.

For champagne bottle, mix flour and water to make a paste. Tear off small strips of newspaper one at a time and dip in paste. Roll strips to form a cylinder 1″ in diameter and 3″ long, tapering gently to 1/2″ diameter for the neck. Let dry thoroughly and paint green. Cut gold foil into strips and wrap around top of bottle, continuing upward to shape a 1/4″-diameter neck and a slightly bulbous cap. Insert and glue bottle at an angle through the hole in the ice. Insert wire through bucket rim; twist to close and clip excess. Thread red cord through wire loop for hanging.

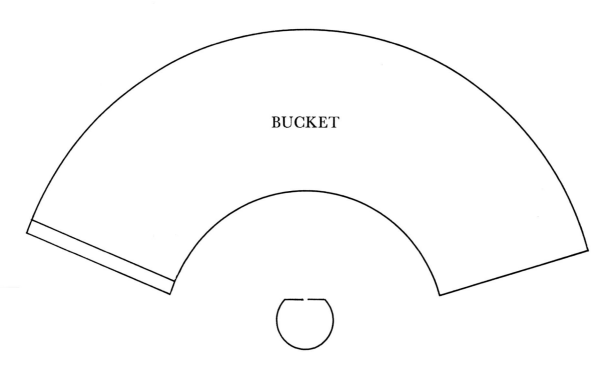

BUCKET

HANDLE DIAGRAM

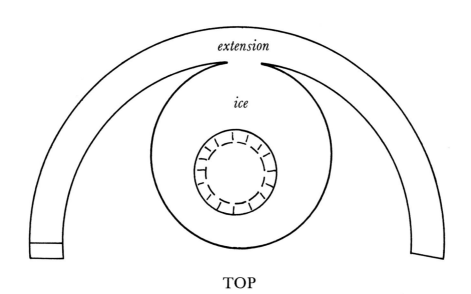

extension

ice

TOP

FAIRYLAND COTTAGE

NOTE: Before beginning, read General Directions for Transferring Designs on page 14.

Skill Level: Intermediate.

Materials: Tracing paper. Mat board 1/16" thick, large piece. Metal-edge ruler. X-acto knife. Scissors. Dowel, 1/16" diameter. Acrylic paints: red, creamy yellow, bright yellow, pine green, kelly green, beige, brown, black. Paintbrush. Craft glue that bonds quickly. Sheet of white paper. Spray adhesive. Iridescent sparkle flakes. Red thread. Sturdy sewing needle.

Directions: Trace patterns. Transfer the following to mat board (be sure to work with white side of board facing outward at all times): one main roof; two pieces for house front/back; two house sides; two vestibules; two vestibule roofs; one chimney; one chimney collar; three large windows; two small windows; one large door; one small door; one wreath; three bushes; three trees; two gate pickets; 85 fence pickets. Using ruler and pencil, draw the following pieces on mat board: one 3 1/4 × 4 3/8" base; two 4 3/8" × 3/4" pieces for base front/back; two 3 1/8 × 3/4" base sides; one 1/4 × 1/2" top step; one 3/8 × 1/2" bottom step; two 1/8 × 3 1/8" side fence supports; two 1/8 × 4 3/8" front/back fence supports. Cut out all pieces using X-acto knife pressed against metal-edge ruler for straight, accurate cuts. Using scissors, cut 3 1/4 × 4 3/8" piece of white paper for base bottom.

Paint mat board pieces as follows: Paint house and vestibules creamy yellow; paint roofs red, extending red for 1/2" onto other side of each piece. Paint doors, shutters, and each side of bushes and trees pine green; paint windows bright yellow. Paint chimney beige with brown bricks; paint chimney collar black. Paint steps brown. Paint wreath kelly green with a red bow. Allow pieces to dry thoroughly.

Assemble base as follows: Glue sides between front and back pieces with outer edges even, making 90° angles. Glue base over sides, making a platform; glue white paper to other side for bottom.

Assemble house as follows: Glue large door to house front with a small window centered above. Glue small door to house back with large window next to door and small window above. Glue large window to each vestibule, centered between sides. Glue house front and back between sides. Score roof on wrong side along center dash line; bend along score for peak of roof. Glue roof to house so eaves extend evenly on each side. Glue house to base, centered between sides and with front set slightly back from one edge. Score wrong side of vestibules and vestibule roofs along dash lines. Bend vestibules along scores and glue, centered, to each side of house and to base. Bend roofs along scores and glue over vestibules, easing notched edges under main house roof. Score chimney and chimney collar along dash lines; bend chimney into a tube and glue securely. Glue collar around top of chimney. Cut two pieces from 1/16" dowel, one 3/8" and one 1/2" long; paint each black, then glue inside chimney collar so that tiny portion is visible. Place chimney on main roof following photograph for position; bevel bottom edges so chimney fits tightly on roof, then glue to roof. Glue large step to base below front door; glue smaller step over large step. Glue trees and bushes to base around house as shown. For fence, glue bottom 1/4" of all pickets to sides of base as follows: Glue four fence pickets centered in front of door, then glue one gate picket on each side of the four center pickets. Glue remainder of pickets, evenly spaced, around entire base. Glue fence supports behind pickets, just above base. Glue wreath to fence between gate pickets.

Spray entire house and base with adhesive. Before adhesive sets, sprinkle house thoroughly with iridescent sparkle flakes; allow to set. For hanger, thread sturdy needle with doubled red thread and run through peak of main roof; tie ends in an overhand knot, making desired size loop. Pick up house by string and shake gently to remove excess flakes.

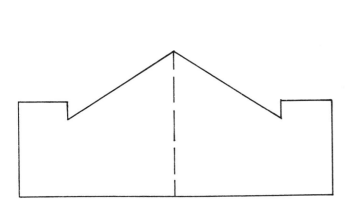

VESTIBULE ROOF

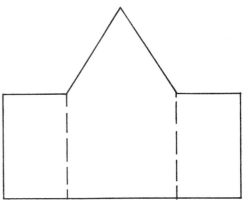

VESTIBULE

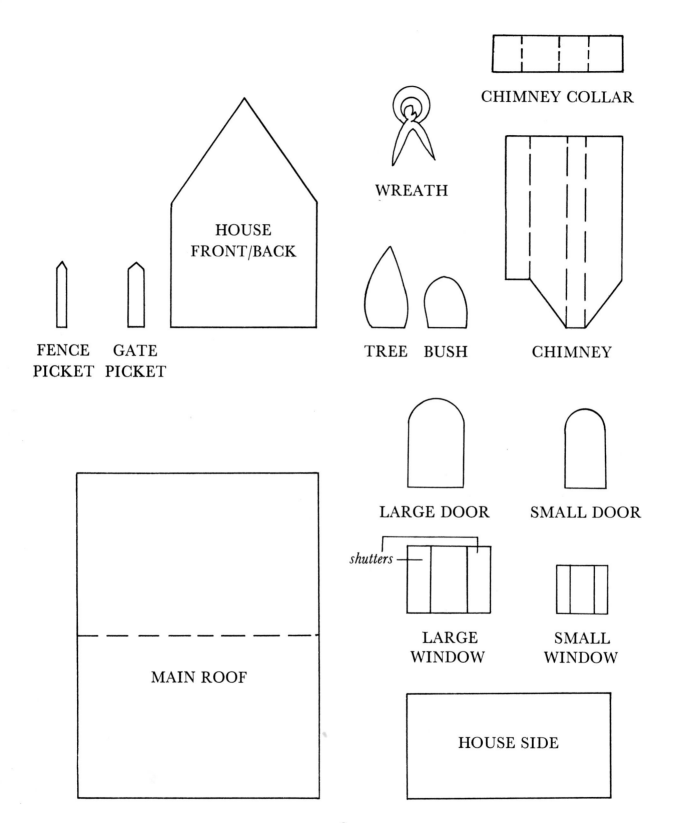

CHIMNEY COLLAR

WREATH

HOUSE
FRONT/BACK

TREE   BUSH

CHIMNEY

FENCE
PICKET

GATE
PICKET

LARGE DOOR

SMALL DOOR

shutters

LARGE
WINDOW

SMALL
WINDOW

MAIN ROOF

HOUSE SIDE

158

Acknowledgments and Craft Credits

The authors and publishers wish to thank several individuals and institutions for their help in preparing this book:

—Bernard J. Murphy of Rochester, N.Y., who graciously shared his Christmas ornament collection with us.
—The companies that so generously lent props for the photographs: F.A.O. Schwarz Fifth Avenue (toys); B. Schackman and Co. (dollhouse furniture); American Tree and Wreath (Christmas decorations); Block China (dishes, stemware, and silverware); Noma Lites, Division of Noma-Worldwide, Inc. (bubble lights); the Swedish Book Nook (the *Julbuk*); and Cepelia Corporation.
—The publishers and authors of three previous works on the subject: Daniel J. Foley, *The Christmas Book* (Chilton, 1960); Philip Snyder, *The Christmas Tree Book* (Viking Penguin, 1977); and Eva Stille, *Christbaumschmuck* (Verlag Hans Carl, Nuremberg, 1979).
—The Scandinavian Tourist Board, the Church of Sweden, and the Ukrainian Museum for their guidance.
—These individuals, who in various ways made important contributions: Miranda Beeson, Lois Brown, Fred Cline, Dr. Hazel Grubbs Davis, Mary Fay, Jane Furth, James Imbriaco, Bob McKee, August Matsdorf, Jr., August Matsdorf, III, Joan Spira, and Don Warning.

Carol Endler Sterbenz: pages 23–27, 33, 35, 39, 42, 59–60, 61–62, 63–64, 65–66, 67–73, 80–81, 82–83, 84–85, 85–86, 86–87, 88, 94–96, 96–97, 98(matzebaum), 99, 100–101, 106–7, 109(Kissing Ball), 116–18, 121–23, 125–27, 133, 136–38, 139–40, 142–43, 150–52, 152–53, 156–58

Nancy Johnson: page 22, 28–29, 33, 34, 40–41, 43, 48–49, 50–54, 54–56, 57–58, 79, 98(pear), 99, 99–100, 105, 109(wreath), 114–15, 118–20, 123–24, 134–35, 140–41, 149, 154–55

Joan Spira: page 89

Index of Ornaments

Make your home special

Since 1922, millions of men and women have turned to *Better Homes and Gardens* magazine for help in making their homes more enjoyable places to be. You, too, can trust *Better Homes and Gardens* to provide you with the best in ideas, inspiration and information for better family living.

In every issue you'll find ideas on food and recipes, decorating and furnishings, crafts and hobbies, remodeling and building, gardening and outdoor living plus family money management, health, education, pets, car maintenance and more.

For information on how you can have *Better Homes and Gardens* delivered to your door, write to: Mr. Robert Austin, P.O. Box 4536, Des Moines, IA 50336.

Better Homes
and Gardens ®

*The Idea Magazine
for Better Homes
and Families*